Reading Comprehension

Teacher Created Materials
PUBLISHING

Teacher Created Materials, Inc.

#10120 Reading Comprehension—Level F

Editor in Chief:
Sharon Coan, M.S. Ed.

Art Director:
Lee Aucoin

Project Managers:
Marcia Russell, M.A. Ed.
Maria Elvira Gallardo, M.A.

Designer:
Lesley Palmer

Product Manager:
Phil Garcia

Product Developers:
Creative Services, Inc.
Teacher Created Materials, Inc.

Photo Credits
Corbis—All except:
    pp. 5,13,49,85,121—Bookmatrix
    pp. 37, 41— Creative Services
    pp. 9,97—Iztli Digital
    p. 33—TCM, Inc.

Publisher
Rachelle Cracchiolo, M.S. Ed.

Teacher Created Materials, Inc.
5301 Oceanus Drive
Huntington Beach, CA 92649-1030
www.tcmpub.com
ISBN-0-7439-0120-7
©2005 Teacher Created Materials, Inc.
Made in U.S.A.

Table of Contents

Introduction to Reading Comprehension

The lessons in this book will help you learn to understand what you read. Each lesson has a selection to read. Then you work with skills to help you understand what you read. Each lesson ends with a practice activity that helps you see what you know about the selection.

You can use these steps to help you as you work in the book. For each selection, follow these steps.

1. Read the Before Reading questions.

> ### Before Reading
> - Do you have brothers or sisters?
> - How are you alike or different from your siblings?

4. Review the selection using the After Reading questions.

> ### After Reading
> - Are there more than these kinds of bikes?
> - Which kind of bike would you like to have?

2. Think about what you already know about the subject.

5. Summarize and apply the information. Complete the activities in the book.

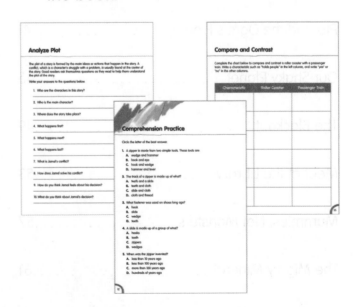

3. Read the During Reading questions.

> ### During Reading
> - How did the brothers get along?
> - How would you feel about moving?

After completing all the activities, use the Comprehension Review section to review the information presented in the book. These pages also help you to check up on your skills.

The Fishing Trip

Mike was scampering down to the lake when he suddenly tripped over something. "Whoa!" Mike yelled, falling hard on the dirt path. As he got up and looked around, he saw that he had fallen over his brother's fishing rod. His brother Eric appeared through the bushes. "Sorry about that," he said, watching Mike dust off his knees. "I was just coming back to get that."

They continued down the overgrown path to the lakeshore, poles and tackle boxes in hand. Their two fishing boats were tied up on the hot sand near an old pier. "Ouch!" Mike exclaimed as he tried to turn his boat over with his hand. "That's one hot boat!" They flipped the boats over with their feet.

Drifting out into the small, shallow lake, they saw their neighbor, Mr. Miffle, who had just hooked something. Eric jumped up in the boat and shouted, "You've got it, Mr. Miffle! Reel it in! Get that fish!" In his excitement, Eric stepped into a metal bucket and lost his balance. He wobbled for a moment or two before falling with a great splash over the side of the boat.

Mike laughed and rowed over to help his dripping, spluttering brother back into the boat. They were both soaked before Eric was finally seated again. Eric glanced sheepishly back at Mr. Miffle, who had put down his reel and was sitting in his boat, arms crossed, a scowl on his face. Eric called out, "Did you get him, Mr. Miffle?"

Mr. Miffle was irate. "No, I didn't," he huffed. "You scared him away with all that shouting and splashing!"

As Eric looked at his brother, he sighed and then grinned. "Maybe we should do something else today," he said. So they paddled back to shore and went in search of another summer adventure.

Before Reading

- When is it important to be quiet?

- Have you ever been in a fishing boat?

During Reading

- How many characters are in the story?

- Where does the story take place?

After Reading

- Were you surprised by what happened? Why or why not?

- Would you shout at a person fishing? Why or why not?

Vocabulary

irate: angry, annoyed

scampering: running playfully

sheepishly: as though embarrassed

spluttering: making spitting or popping noises

shallow: not deep

scowl: an angry look

Identify Cause and Effect

Fill in the missing cause and effect in the chart. Then write two other cause-effect relationships in the space provided.

Cause	Effect
Eric left his fishing rod in the path.	
	Mike's hand was burned.

Identify Story Elements

Summarize the different elements of "The Fishing Trip" in the chart.

The Fishing Trip	
Setting: When and where did the story happen?	
Characters: Who are the characters? What did you learn about them?	
Plot: What is the important action of the story?	

Comprehension Practice

Circle the letter of the best answer.

1. Why did Mike trip on the path?
   A. His shoe was untied.
   B. A tree branch was in the way.
   C. Eric had left his fishing pole on the path.
   D. Mike is very clumsy.

2. What burns Mike's hand?
   A. the sand
   B. the boat
   C. rocks
   D. water

3. What is Mr. Miffle doing when the brothers see him?
   A. swimming toward them
   B. shouting at them
   C. rescuing a swimmer
   D. reeling in a fish

4. What is the main reason Eric falls out of the boat?
   A. He is shouting.
   B. He steps in a bucket.
   C. He trips on a fishing rod.
   D. His brother splashed him.

5. When does this story most likely take place?
   A. in the winter
   B. during a rainstorm
   C. in the summer
   D. late at night

Get That Bug

Before Reading

- How do cats like to play?
- Why is it important to learn from our mistakes?

During Reading

- Who is the main character?
- What happens when Junior doesn't listen to Mrs. Lubsy?

After Reading

- Why do you think cats sneak up on things?
- Do you think Junior will listen to Mrs. Lubsy in the future?

Mrs. Lubsy's cat, Junior, loves to chase bugs. Recently Mrs. Lubsy told me about one of Junior's adventures. Junior had noticed a tiny bug hovering above the dresser. He closely watched the gnat as it flew in circles. Mrs. Lubsy saw him glaring at the insect and said, "Don't you try to get that bug! Remember what happened last time? You'll jump and swat and wreck the whole house!" But Junior kept on watching. He wanted to jump up and catch that bug.

The tiny bug flew higher and higher. Junior's head moved in circles as he stared at the bug. Over her magazine, Mrs. Lubsy watched him eyeing the insect. "Why do you have to chase everything?" she asked. "Playing with a tiny gnat? You look ridiculous." But Junior just sat there staring. He sure did want to swat the tiny, uninvited guest.

Junior locked his sights on the tiny gnat and crouched. Suddenly, he pounced at the little bug. He took off like a little rocket and landed on Mrs. Lubsy's dresser. He swatted with his left and his right paws, but the little gnat just hovered over him. Things on the dresser went flying while Mrs. Lubsy shouted, "Get down from there, you ridiculous cat!"

Junior didn't get that bug. Instead, he slid off the dresser and crashed to the floor. He then quietly walked out and curled up in the laundry basket. He sure wanted to get that bug.

Vocabulary

gnat: tiny fly

hover: stay in one place in the air

ridiculous: absurd or laughable

Visualize

Picture each scene in your mind. Write details about what you see.

1. Junior locked his sights on the tiny gnat and crouched. Suddenly, he pounced at the little bug. He took off like a little rocket and landed on Mrs. Lubsy's dresser.

_____

_____

_____

_____

_____

_____

2. The tiny bug flew higher and higher. Junior's head moved in circles as he stared at the bug.

_____

_____

_____

_____

_____

_____

#10120 Reading Comprehension—Level F   Teacher Created Materials, Inc.

Analyze Plot Structure

Identify the parts of the plot for "Get That Bug."

Conflict (problem or main dilemma)

_____

_____

_____

_____

Action Leading to Solving the Problem

_____

_____

_____

_____

Resolution (outcome or how the story ends)

_____

_____

_____

_____

Comprehension Practice

Circle the letter of the best answer.

1. In the story, who is Junior?
   A. Mrs. Lubsy's son
   B. Mrs. Lubsy's cat
   C. the narrator of the story
   D. a bug

2. What was Junior staring at?
   A. a fish
   B. a fly
   C. a gnat
   D. a string

3. What happened when Mrs. Lubsy told Junior not to get the bug?
   A. He went away.
   B. He sat by her.
   C. He didn't listen.
   D. The bug flew away.

4. What was Mrs. Lubsy doing at the time the story takes place?
   A. dusting the dresser
   B. washing dishes
   C. watching television
   D. reading

5. Where did Junior go after he fell?
   A. the laundry basket
   B. the pantry
   C. his food dish
   D. under the sofa

Tiny Santi

Before Reading

- What might it be like to be the size of a mouse?
- What would a mouse be afraid of?

During Reading

- Where does the story take place?
- What happens to Santi?

After Reading

- If you could make yourself mouse-sized, what would you do?
- What did you think was going to happen to Santi?

Santi's big brother Len had told him never to push all the remote control buttons at the same time. He said that something terrible would happen if he did.

Santi didn't really believe this. While Len was out of the room, Santi plopped down on the couch with the remote in his hand. For a while, he flipped from channel to channel, looking for something interesting to watch. Bored, Santi decided to see what Len could have meant. With a

quick glance over his shoulder to make sure Len hadn't come back, he pushed all the buttons at once.

Santi saw a bright flash, and he dropped the remote control. "I've broken it," he thought. "Now I'm in trouble!" As he looked around for the remote control, he realized he was in more trouble than he'd thought. He was suddenly only the size of a mouse!

"Oh, no!" Santi squeaked. He had to find his parents quickly. Carefully, he climbed down the side of the gigantic couch and scurried across the floor. In the kitchen, Santi could see that the sliding door had been left open. "If the door's open, then the cat might be in here," tiny Santi said.

Just then, Santi and the cat spotted each other. Santi ran for the door, the cat closing in quickly behind him. Just as the cat reached out to swat Santi, it slipped on some water and slid across the kitchen floor. Out of breath, Santi ducked behind a flowerpot on the porch.

He could see his mom far away in the garden. "How will I ever get there?" he wondered. As he peeked out from behind the flowerpot, there was the huge cat looking right at him! Santi darted for the garden and then . . . he woke up. "It was only a dream!" he said with a relieved laugh. "Thank goodness!"

Vocabulary

relieved: no longer having fear or worry

remote: controlled from a distance

scurried: moved quickly

Identify Story Elements

Summarize the different elements of "Tiny Santi" in the chart.

Tiny Santi	
Setting: When and where did the story happen?	
Characters: Who are the characters? What did you learn about them?	
Plot: What is the important action of the story?	

 #10120 Reading Comprehension—Level F   *Teacher Created Materials, Inc.*

Identify Cause and Effect

Fill in the missing cause and effect in the chart. Then write two other cause-effect relationships in the space provided.

Cause	Effect
	Santi shrank to the size of a mouse.
The sliding door was left open.	

Comprehension Practice

1. What did Santi's brother say would happen if he pushed all the remote control buttons?
   A. something terrible
   B. He would turn into a mouse.
   C. something funny
   D. He would shrink.

2. What was the first thing Santi did after shrinking himself?
   A. He ran from the cat.
   B. He went to find his parents.
   C. He hid behind a flowerpot.
   D. He woke up.

3. Why did Santi suspect the cat was in the kitchen?
   A. He heard a mouse squeaking.
   B. His mom kept the cat in the kitchen.
   C. The sliding door had been left open.
   D. He could hear it.

4. Where was Santi's mom?
   A. at work
   B. in the kitchen
   C. in the garage
   D. in the garden

5. How did Santi escape the cat the second time?
   A. He reached his mom in the garden.
   B. He woke up.
   C. He scared the cat away.
   D. He jumped into the flowerpot.

Randy and the Blustery Day

One blustery day, Randy was flying his kite up on Balmy Hill. Suddenly, a tremendous gust of wind ran up the hill and lifted Randy right off his feet! Randy grasped the kite string tightly as the great wind carried him over the town, across fields and rivers, and through the clouds. In time, the wind finally guided Randy's kite back down to Earth.

Randy landed beside a dusty road. He wound up his kite string and walked down the road until he came to a sign outside a small town. The sign read, "Nowhere: The Town Nobody's Ever Heard Of." This worried Randy.

Before Reading

- What do you know about wind?
- What kinds of things can wind do?

During Reading

- Where does the story take place?
- Is the story real or make-believe?

After Reading

- In what ways is this story similar to real life?
- What do you think happened when Randy got home?

He stopped in a little store and asked the clerk where he was. "Nowhere, of course" was the answer.

"Where is Nowhere?" Randy asked.

"How should I know?" the clerk replied. "Nobody knows." This worried Randy even more. He went from place to place, asking people where Nowhere was. But everyone gave him the same answer: "How should I know where Nowhere is? Nobody knows."

Then Randy saw a very important-looking man strolling down the road, and he heard the townspeople whispering that he was the Grand Duke. Randy ran to him and asked, "Sir, where is Nowhere?" The Grand Duke, looking a bit surprised, answered, "I am clearly not Nobody, so obviously I have no idea. But since you are asking, then you must have come from Somewhere. I will send you back."

The Grand Duke clapped his hands twice. A great wind came up and pulled the kite, along with Randy, into the clouds and back to Balmy Hill, just in time for dinner.

Vocabulary

blustery: extremely windy

obviously: clearly

tremendous: of extreme power or greatness

Predict

Before and during reading, use your own knowledge and imagination to predict what is going to happen next in the story.

1. Read the title of the story, and then stop. Write down what you think this story is going to be about. Why do you think so?

    _____

    _____

    _____

2. Read the first paragraph of the story, and then stop. Write your prediction about what is going to happen to Randy.

    _____

    _____

    _____

3. When you finish reading, check your predictions. How do your predictions compare to the story? Are your predictions more or less realistic than the story?

    _____

    _____

    _____

Analyze Plot Structure

Fill in the chart. Identify the elements of the plot.

Conflict/Problem
Action Leading to Solving the Problem
Resolution/Outcome

Comprehension Practice

Circle the letter of the best answer.

1. Where was Randy flying his kite?
   A. at home
   B. in town
   C. on a hill
   D. by the river

2. Where did Randy finally land?
   A. on his family's farm
   B. by a dusty road
   C. by the Grand Duke's palace
   D. on a different hill

3. Who was the first person Randy met in Nowhere?
   A. a store clerk
   B. the Grand Duke
   C. a police officer
   D. a postman

4. What is the Grand Duke's reaction to Randy's question?
   A. confusion because he could not understand Randy
   B. worry about Randy's safety
   C. surprise at being asked such a question
   D. excitement because of Randy's adventure

5. Where does the Duke suppose Randy must be from?
   A. Nowhere
   B. Balmy Hill
   C. a little town outside Nowhere
   D. Somewhere

Marvin Comes to Stay

Robert had just turned on his bathwater when David, his older brother, came running in. "Look what I got," he told Robert, and he pulled out a little frog he'd been hiding in his shirt.

Before Reading

- What do you know about frogs?

- Why is it important to look after pets?

During Reading

- Will their mom find the frog before the boys do?

- What happens when the frog gets away from David?

After Reading

- What do you think happens when the boys find Marvin in the tub?

- Do you think the boys will still want to keep Marvin? Why or why not?

"His name's Marvin," David said. The boys figured their mom wouldn't mind the frog as long as they kept it in a tank. Marvin didn't give them a chance to find a suitable tank. Without warning, the frog leaped to the floor and out the door. "Uh-oh!" they exclaimed together. "Catch him!"

"We can't let Mom find him," David warned. Surprised at how quick the frog was, the boys chased the pocket-sized creature down the staircase. On his hands and knees, David crept after the elusive frog.

As the boys gave chase, Marvin hopped under shelves and behind furniture. Just when the boys thought they had it, the critter sprang from behind the TV. When they thought they'd cornered it in the dining room, it bounded through their fingers.

Under the coffee table the frog went, just as Robert dove across the carpet. It hopped onto the green couch, seemingly to camouflage itself, and then disappeared. "Where'd he go?" Robert whispered.

"I don't know," David frowned. "He was just here." They frantically searched under the cushions.

A moment later, Mom called from the garage. "Robert, your bathwater is probably cold by now," she said. The tub! The boys bounded up the staircase to the bathroom. There in the bathtub, they found that the water had cooled. Swimming happily in the cool water was their sneaky amphibious friend Marvin.

Vocabulary

amphibious: able to live both on land and in water

camouflage: disguise

elusive: hard to catch or find

Identify Author's Purpose and Viewpoint

Authors write for many different reasons. Think about why the author wrote "Marvin Comes to Stay." Then answer the questions.

1. What is the subject of the story?

   _____

2. Does this story tell facts about the subject?

   _____

3. Does this story mostly entertain?

   _____

4. Does the story try to persuade you to do something?

   _____

5. Does the story try to persuade you to believe something?

   _____

6. Think about your answers to questions 1–5. Then circle the reason why the author wrote the article. Explain on the lines below.

       to entertain   to inform   to persuade

   _____

   _____

   _____

Identify Story Elements

Fill in the chart. Identify the elements of the plot.

Characters

Setting

Conflict/Problem

Resolution/Outcome

Comprehension Practice

Circle the letter of the best answer.

1. Who was running bathwater?
   A. David
   B. Robert
   C. Marvin
   D. Mom

2. Where did the boys plan to keep Marvin?
   A. in the bathtub
   B. in the sink
   C. in David's shirt pocket
   D. in a tank

3. What is one thing about Marvin that caught both boys by surprise?
   A. He was quicker than they were.
   B. He could jump.
   C. He liked to swim.
   D. He was small.

4. Why was the couch like camouflage?
   A. It had a jungle pattern.
   B. It was the same color as Marvin.
   C. It was too low for the boys to look under it.
   D. It was in a dark room.

5. What made the boys think of looking in the bathtub?
   A. They heard a splash as Marvin jumped in.
   B. They were going to wash their hands for dinner.
   C. Marvin had snuck into the bathroom before.
   D. Mom reminded Robert that the water was getting cold.

A Star's Life

An exploding star

Where do stars come from? Do they age? What happens to them over time?

A galaxy has clouds of dust and gas. Here stars are born. Gravity pulls more and more gas into a cloud. The cloud begins to spin. Particles of gas bump into each other faster and faster. This creates energy, and the cloud gets hotter. Finally, the cloud gets so hot that atoms are joined, and the cloud begins to glow. This growing, glowing cloud of gas is a protostar. A protostar becomes a main sequence star when it stops growing. Main sequence stars can shine for millions of years, depending on how big they are.

An average-sized star will begin to shrink when its fuel is used. This happens because gravity pulls the remaining matter closer together. In fact, the star could shrink to just a few hundred miles or kilometers wide! This star, called a white dwarf, can stay like this for a long time. At some time, however, it will stop producing light. It then is a black dwarf, which floats in space forever.

Matter in large stars continues to join and get hotter until iron forms. Iron acts like a sponge. It soaks up the star's energy. In time, this energy is released in a huge explosion called a supernova. The bit of matter that was once at the center of the star becomes either a neutron star or a black hole. A star that was several times larger than our sun becomes a neutron star. If it was larger than that, it becomes a black hole.

Before Reading

- What is in space?
- What are stars?

During Reading

- Where are stars born?
- What happens after a star explodes?

After Reading

- What is the sequence of life for stars?
- How do people learn about stars?

Vocabulary

galaxy: a huge group of stars and gases

protostar: a glowing cloud of gas that becomes a star

stars: huge balls of gas that give off heat and light

supernova: the explosion of a large star

white dwarf: a shrunken star

Identify Sequence

List in order the events that take place in the life of a star. Begin with the birth of the star and finish with the final phases of a black dwarf, neutron star, or black hole.

Star Sequence of Events

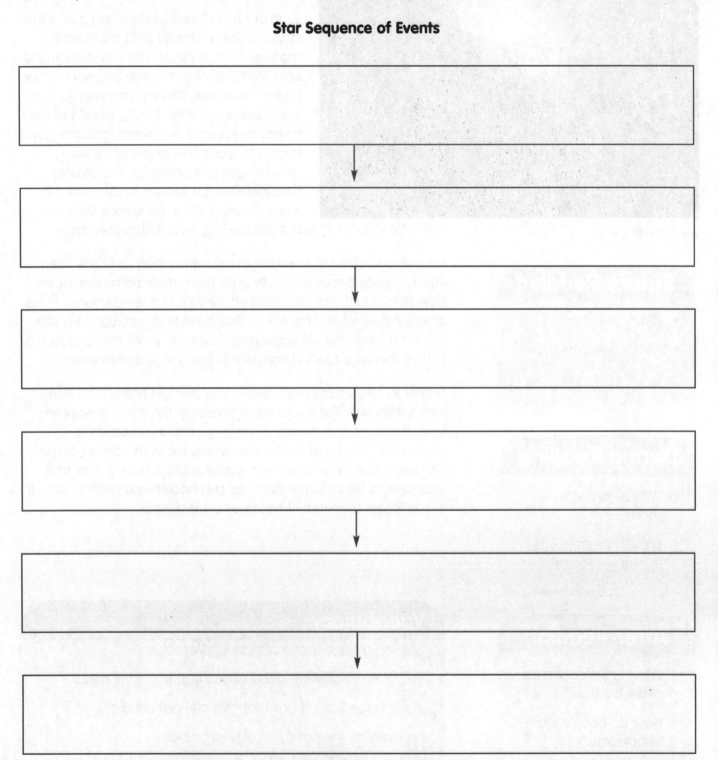

Identify Cause and Effect

Answer the following questions about cause and effect. Remember a cause is why something happens and an effect is what happens.

1. A protostar is formed when atoms are joined together and release tremendous energy. What causes the atoms to join together?

    _____

    _____

    _____

2. What causes a star to become a black dwarf?

    _____

    _____

    _____

3. What effect does iron have on a star?

    _____

    _____

    _____

4. In time, huge stars become either neutron stars or black holes. What causes this to happen to a star?

    _____

    _____

    _____

Comprehension Practice

Circle the letter of the best answer.

1. What pulls gas and dust into a cloud?
   A. galaxy
   B. heat
   C. gravity
   D. light

2. What determines how long a star will shine?
   A. space
   B. size
   C. weight
   D. brightness

3. In the average star, what happens when its fuel is used up?
   A. It melts.
   B. It floats away.
   C. It stops moving.
   D. It shrinks.

4. What is the last stage of life for an average-sized star?
   A. black dwarf
   B. black hole
   C. neutron star
   D. black matter

5. What is the explosion of a huge star called?
   A. white dwarf
   B. supernova
   C. sun
   D. protostar

 #10120 Reading Comprehension—Level F Teacher Created Materials, Inc.

Kenny's Great Story

Before Reading

- What are dreams?
- Why do you think people write stories?

One Friday, Mrs. Melba asked her class to write a story. "Use your imagination!" she cried. "You can write your story about anything."

Kenny looked confused. "A story?" he thought. "What could I possibly have to write about? I don't know any stories." The bell rang to announce the end of the school day. All the kids took their backpacks and went home.

The next day, Kenny sat on the couch with a pad of paper and pen in hand. He tried to think of a story to write for Mrs. Melba. He thought and thought, and then he thought some more.

"I just don't have any imagination," he thought to himself. "I cannot think of a single thing to write as a story."

The warm sun was shining through the window, making him drowsy. Kenny sat there thinking and thinking, and soon he nodded off and fell fast asleep. As he slept, Kenny began to dream about fantastic things.

First he dreamed that he was a world-famous doctor, saving whole cities and curing diseases. Then he dreamed that he was in a UFO, talking to strange but friendly space creatures. Then he dreamed that he had been shrunk to the size of a mouse by an evil scientist. In his tiny state, he had to find a way to foil the plot of the mad scientist!

Kenny dreamed wonderful and exciting things until his little brother woke him up.

"What were you dreaming about?" he asked.

Kenny told his brother the wonderful dreams. His brother enjoyed the stories. Suddenly, Kenny knew that he had all kinds of stories in his imagination. He could write about one of his dreams!

During Reading

- Where does the story take place?
- What happens when Kenny falls asleep?

After Reading

- Did you think Kenny was going to think of a story? Why or why not?
- Which of Kenny's dreams would you write a story about?

Vocabulary

drowsy: sleepy

fantastic: incredible, unbelievable

foil: to ruin; to spoil

imagination: the ability to create images in one's mind

Analyze Plot Structure

Fill in the chart. Identify the elements of the plot.

Conflict/Problem
Action Leading to Solving the Problem
Resolution/Outcome

Visualize

1. Read the third, fourth, and fifth paragraphs of the selection. Picture all the parts of this scene in your mind. Write about what you see.

    _____

    _____

    _____

    _____

2. Choose one of Kenny's dreams. Draw a picture showing what you picture in your mind when you read the description.

Comprehension Practice

Circle the letter of the best answer.

1. On what day was Kenny working on his assignment?
   A. Monday
   B. Thursday
   C. Friday
   D. Saturday

2. Where was Kenny doing his homework?
   A. at his desk
   B. on the couch
   C. on his bed
   D. on the back porch

3. What made Kenny sleepy?
   A. warm sunlight
   B. thinking too much
   C. staying up too late
   D. drinking warm milk

4. What was Kenny in his first dream?
   A. a mad scientist
   B. a visitor on a spaceship
   C. shrunken
   D. a great doctor

5. Who woke Kenny up?
   A. Mrs. Melba
   B. his mom
   C. his little brother
   D. his older brother

Two of a Kind

Jim and Joe are twins. They both have brown hair and blue eyes and are pretty much identical. Joe always wears a blue baseball cap so their friends can tell them apart. Jim never wears one because he prefers football.

One day, their friend Kate invited them to an ice-skating party. They put on heavy brown sweaters, and Jim wore a plaid scarf. Joe put his blue cap in his back pocket and they went off to the ice rink.

When they arrived, Jim and Joe saw that they were the first ones there. They rented their skates and put them on. Jim's skates were black and Joe's were red with a white stripe. They supposed they would hop on the ice and skate until their friends showed up.

A few minutes later, Kate arrived and rented skates without delay. As she dashed onto the ice, she immediately met Jim and Joe. Just as she was about to say hello to them, she realized she didn't know which was Jim or which was Joe! Jim laughed and put the ball cap on Joe's head.

After a few laps, they joined the others at the party table for ice cream. Jim took chocolate, but Joe and Kate chose vanilla. Everybody talked and talked, mostly about school. Jim and some others liked math best, while Joe enjoyed history. Kate and Jim talked about playing saxophone in the school band, while Joe and a few kids talked about their drum lessons.

When all the ice cream had been gobbled up, everybody scampered onto the ice and skated the rest of the day.

Before Reading

- What are some things that look alike?

- Have you ever been ice-skating?

During Reading

- Where are the brothers going?

- How are the two brothers different?

After Reading

- Why is it good for people to have differences?

- How are things you like different from what your friends like?

Vocabulary

identical: having the same appearance

plaid: a crisscross pattern of multicolored stripes of different widths

rink: a surface for ice-skating or roller-skating

Analyze Characters

Write down similarities and differences of the two main characters, Jim and Joe, in "Two of a Kind."

Jim	Joe

How Jim and Joe are alike:

         Teacher Created Materials, Inc.

Identify Sequence

Write the events below in the order in which they occurred.

Kate arrived at the skating rink and rented skates.

Jim put the cap on Joe's head so that Kate could tell them apart.

Kate invited Jim and Joe to a party.

Everyone skated for a while.

Jim and Joe went to the skating rink and started skating.

The kids had ice cream and chatted.

Jim put on a plaid scarf.

1.

2.

3.

4.

5.

6.

7.

Comprehension Practice

Circle the letter of the best answer.

1. Why doesn't Jim wear a baseball cap?
   A. Joe doesn't like for him to wear caps.
   B. It wouldn't match his scarf.
   C. He prefers football.
   D. He lost his cap.

2. Where did Joe put his baseball cap before they left for the party?
   A. on his head
   B. on Jim's head
   C. in his backpack
   D. in his back pocket

3. What happened when Jim and Joe got to the ice rink?
   A. Kate asked them to leave.
   B. They started skating because they were early.
   C. They rented their skates.
   D. Joe gave his hat to Jim to trick everyone else.

4. What were the kids talking mostly about at the table?
   A. school
   B. sports teams
   C. ice skating
   D. a recent rock concert

5. What is Jim's favorite class at school?
   A. gym
   B. history
   C. music
   D. math

Up in the Attic

Billy's mom had been asking him to clean the attic for months. One Saturday, Billy was bored and decided it was time to get the job done. He walked up the dusty stairs, pushed open the old door, and got right to work.

As Billy sifted through boxes, shuffled through papers, dusted, and cleaned, he found all sorts of odd little treasures. He found funny pictures of his parents when they were younger, old toys of every description, and many books. Billy found some of his own toys and clothes from when he was much younger. He smiled. The attic certainly had lots of stories to tell about his family.

A small wooden box, tucked in the far corner of the attic, caught Billy's eye. He went over and opened it. In it he found some old papers. One looked like a map. As he looked closely at it, Billy discovered that the map showed a house—his house! Then Billy realized that, whatever the map led to, it led right to his own bedroom!

He ran back down the stairs with the map in hand. He was very excited now and sped into his room to find what he was sure would be a wonderful surprise. As he opened the door to his room, he smelled the aroma of his favorite thing in the world: banana nut muffins. There, on the corner of his desk, was a plate of warm muffins and a tall glass of cold milk. Beside the plate was a note from his mom. "Thank you for cleaning the attic," it said. "I hope you enjoy this little treasure too! Love, Mom."

Vocabulary

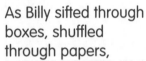

aroma: a smell that is usually pleasant

attic: a room or space below a building's roof

treasure: an item of value

Before Reading

- What are attics for?
- What chores do your parents ask you to do at home?

During Reading

- What happens when Billy starts cleaning?
- Where do you think the map will lead to?

After Reading

- What do you think will happen next time Billy is asked to clean the attic?
- Were you surprised at the end? Why or why not?

Make Inferences

Use what you read in "Up in the Attic" and what you already know to make some inferences about the story.

		What I Read	What I Know	My Inference
1.	When did Billy's mom put the map in the attic?			
2.	Did Billy agree that the map led to a treasure?			
3.	How did Billy's mom know he would find the map?			
4.	What kind of kid does Billy seem to be?			

#10120 Reading Comprehension—Level F   Teacher Created Materials, Inc.

Identify Story Elements

Summarize the different elements of "Up in the Attic" in the chart.

Up in the Attic	
Setting: When and where did the story happen?	
Characters: Who are the characters? What did you learn about them?	
Plot: What is the important action of the story?	

Comprehension Practice

Circle the letter of the best answer.

1. Why did Billy clean the attic?
   A. His dad told him to.
   B. He was bored.
   C. He wanted some muffins.
   D. He enjoys cleaning.

2. What did Billy not find in the attic?
   A. funny pictures
   B. a map
   C. old toys
   D. muffins

3. Where did Billy find the treasure map?
   A. in a cardboard box
   B. under a loose board
   C. in a small wooden box
   D. on the corner of his desk

4. Where did Billy think the treasure was hidden?
   A. under the wooden box
   B. in his bedroom
   C. in the kitchen
   D. behind the garage

5. What is Billy's favorite treat?
   A. banana nut muffins
   B. milk
   C. chocolate chip cookies
   D. blueberry muffins

Pip and the Ogre's Frog

Long ago, in a barren, long-forgotten place called the Land Beyond, a boy planted food for his masters. His name was Pip, and his masters were 12 mean and nasty ogres. Under the three hot suns of this land, Pip planted bunclecorn. It was the only thing that would grow. Every day, day after day, Pip toiled in the fields.

Every night, night after night, Pip dreamed of leaving the Land Beyond. He imagined that he was in a faraway place with trees, water, and animals. Most of all, he dreamed of living with kind people.

One night, Pip dared to sneak away. As he crossed the fields that he had tended day after day, a frog jumped into his path. The frog belonged to the meanest and nastiest ogre. Pip feared that he would call out to his master, but he did not. The frog begged to go with Pip. He wanted to return to the forest where his family lived. Pip agreed and put the frog in his sack.

Pip walked on day after day under the three suns and night after night beneath the purple moon. The frog's family lived far from the Land Beyond, but Pip plodded onward.

At long last, Pip came to a lush forest where a great and mighty river flowed. This was Frog's home. Frog sprang from Pip's bag and was soon back with his family.

Joyous at the return of his son, Father Frog insisted on rewarding Pip. Suddenly, a tidy cottage appeared on the cliffs. Behind it was a village bustling with activity. Frog's father gave Pip the cottage. Pip lived there happily, growing vegetables and eventually raising a family of his own.

Before Reading

- What makes a story a fantasy?
- What is an ogre?

During Reading

- How do the Land Beyond and the frog's home differ?
- Why was Pip rewarded? Did he deserve the reward?

After Reading

- Were you surprised by what happened at the end? Why or why not?
- How can you tell that this story is a fantasy?

Vocabulary

barren: having few plants

ogre: a large, mean giant

plodded: walked in a slow and heavy way

cottage: a small house

toil: to work hard

Analyze Characters

1. What does Pip do in the Land Beyond?

_____

_____

2. What does Pip long for the most?

_____

_____

3. Is Pip resigned to his life as a servant to the ogres?

_____

_____

4. How does Pip respond to Frog? What does this response tell about Pip's character?

_____

_____

5. Was Pip willing to struggle to achieve his goal?

_____

_____

6. Choose three of the following words. Tell how they apply to Pip.

hardworking   determined   thoughtful   helpful
happy   brave   sad   kind

_____

_____

_____

_____

Visualize

Imagine what Pip's new home will look like. Draw a picture of his new home in the box. Then describe your picture and what Pip will do in his new home. Write a short paragraph on the lines below to accompany your picture.

_____

_____

_____

_____

_____

_____

_____

Comprehension Practice

Circle the letter of the best answer.

1. Why did Pip grow only bunclecorn?
   A. It was the only food the ogres would eat.
   B. The ogres could make a lot of money selling bunclecorn in the marketplace.
   C. Bunclecorn was the only crop that would grow on the barren land.
   D. Bunclecorn required less sunshine than other crops.

2. How many ogres were Pip's masters?
   A. three
   B. six
   C. ten
   D. twelve

3. Why was Pip fearful that the frog would call for his master?
   A. The master would force Pip to return to his work in the fields.
   B. The noise would frighten Pip.
   C. The master would want to go with Pip.
   D. Pip didn't think the frog's master would hear him.

4. What word best describes Pip during his walk to Frog's home?
   A. careless
   B. lazy
   C. kind
   D. selfish

5. What was the frog's home most like?
   A. the Land Beyond
   B. the land of Pip's dream
   C. a barren land where only bunclecorn grew
   D. the ogres' homeland

Our Shaky Planet

Earthquakes can cause great destruction

Parts of Earth are always moving. The movements are usually so small and so slow that we can't feel them. Whole mountains and even continents move. For example, even as you read this, the continents of North America and Europe are moving away from each other. We don't feel it because continents move only about as fast as your fingernails grow.

Sometimes, though, we can see and feel the movements. Sections of Earth's crust push against each other. Where they meet is called a fault. If the sections cannot pass easily, the earth bends and buckles under the surface. When the pressure and friction of this buckled rock releases its energy, a whole section of Earth's crust may move four or five feet at once. The huge vibrations caused by this are called seismic waves. These waves are what we feel as earthquakes.

Every day, there are thousands of earthquakes around the world. Most are small and harmless, but some are very dangerous. In a small earthquake, dishes might rattle and ceiling lights might swing. The ground jiggles a bit, as if a big truck were going by. In a big earthquake, buildings may fall. Pipes that carry water and gas can be broken, causing fires. Dams, bridges, and roadways may buckle and break. Large earthquakes can cause landslides and huge waves called tsunamis, which can cause great damage.

Scientists know a lot about earthquakes. They know what causes them. They can tell how strong they are. Maybe one day they will even be able to predict earthquakes.

Vocabulary

buckles: folds and breaks

fault: point where two sections of Earth's crust meet

seismic waves: vibrations caused by movements of Earth's crust

tsunami: a giant ocean wave caused by an earthquake

Before Reading

- What is an earthquake?
- What do you know about earthquakes?

During Reading

- What causes earthquakes?
- Why don't we feel some earthquakes?

After Reading

- Do you think science will ever be able to stop earthquakes?
- How do you think cities might be made safer from earthquakes?

Make Inferences

Use what you read in "Our Shaky Planet" and what you already know to make some inferences about Earth and earthquakes.

	What I Read	What I Know	My Inference
1. Where is Earth's crust?			
2. How much energy is released in an earthquake?			
3. Why are earthquakes near cities more dangerous?			
4. If more than 1,000 earthquakes happen each day, why do we not hear about them more often?			

#10120 Reading Comprehension—Level F   Teacher Created Materials, Inc.

Summarize and Paraphrase

Paraphrasing means restating something you read in your own words. Paraphrasing can help you understand and remember what you read. Read each of the following passages from "Our Shaky Planet" and rewrite them in your own words.

1. From the article:	2. From the article:
Parts of Earth are always moving. The movements are usually so small and so slow that we can't feel them. Whole mountains and even continents move. We don't feel it because continents move only about as fast as your fingernails grow.	If the sections cannot pass easily, the earth bends and buckles under the surface. When the pressure and friction of this buckled rock releases its energy, a whole section of Earth's crust may move four or five feet at once. The huge vibrations caused by this are called seismic waves.
1. Your paraphrase:	**2. Your paraphrase:**

Comprehension Practice

Circle the letter of the best answer.

1. How fast do most sections of Earth's crust ordinarily move?
   A. four or five feet in a few seconds
   B. several miles per day
   C. about as fast as a fingernail grows
   D. They don't move unless there's an earthquake.

2. What is a fault?
   A. an earthquake that causes little damage
   B. a huge ocean wave caused by an earthquake
   C. the outer layer of Earth
   D. an area where two sections of Earth's crust meet

3. When seismic waves are felt on Earth's surface, it is called _____.
   A. an earthquake
   B. a fault
   C. continental motion
   D. a jiggler

4. About how many earthquakes occur every day?
   A. 100
   B. 5
   C. 500
   D. 1,000

5. Which of the following would be least likely to happen during a small earthquake?
   A. Dishes in a cabinet rattle.
   B. The ground jiggles a little bit.
   C. Large buildings collapse.
   D. Ceiling lights and hanging signs swing.

The Blackout

Before Reading

- How do you have fun with your parents?
- How do you work with your parents?

During Reading

- What made it difficult to get around in the dark?
- Where does the story take place?

After Reading

- What did you think was going to happen in the story?
- Why was it good that Gerald helped his dad in the basement?

Vocabulary

adjusted: got used to

fuse: a safety device that controls how much electricity runs through a wire

One day, Gerald was helping his dad clean the basement. His dad was running an old, noisy air conditioner to see if it still worked. Suddenly, a fuse blew and the lights went out. Gerald stayed still until his eyes adjusted to the darkness.

There were boxes full of all kinds of old junk piled up all over the floor. This made it very hard for Gerald and his dad to get around in the dark. His dad hadn't been wearing his glasses and couldn't see a thing. Trying to get to where he thought he'd put a flashlight, he tripped and fell into a huge box. Gerald found the flashlight and pointed it at his dad.

With the flashlight, they saw that the big box was full of old pictures. They began sorting through the pictures and having quite a time. Gerald found a photo of the time their pool sprang a leak and flooded the lawn. His dad found some photos from when he was just a little kid.

As they picked through the box, a light came down from the top of the stairs and they heard some clicking sounds. Suddenly all the lights came back on! Gerald's mom had come home and replaced the fuse for them.

With all the lights back on, they could see that the huge box was filled with hundreds of pictures and movies they had made as a family. They decided to look through all the pictures and home movies after dinner and have a fun evening.

Predict

Before and during reading, use your own knowledge and imagination to predict what is going to happen next in the story.

1. Read the title of the story, then stop. Write down what you think this story is going to be about. Why do you think so?

   _____

   _____

   _____

2. Read the first paragraph of the story, then stop. Write your prediction about what is going to happen to Gerald and his dad.

   _____

   _____

   _____

3. Read the second and third paragraphs, then stop. What do you think is going to happen when the lights come back on?

   _____

   _____

   _____

4. When you finish reading, check your predictions. How do your predictions compare to the story? Are your predictions more or less realistic than the story?

   _____

   _____

   _____

Identify Cause and Effect

Fill in the missing cause and effect in the chart. Then write two other cause-effect relationships in the space provided.

Cause	Effect
	A fuse blew and the lights went out.
Dad wasn't wearing his glasses, and it was too dark to see where he was walking.	

Comprehension Practice

Circle the letter of the best answer.

1. What was Gerald doing when the lights went out?
   A. fixing an air conditioner
   B. looking for a flashlight
   C. cleaning the basement
   D. looking for the fuse box

2. What was all over the floor?
   A. water
   B. boxes
   C. bags of pictures
   D. garbage

3. Why couldn't Gerald's dad see?
   A. It was late at night.
   B. He didn't have his glasses.
   C. He didn't have a fuse.
   D. He couldn't find the light switch.

4. Gerald found a picture of what?
   A. his class field trip
   B. the flooded lawn
   C. his father
   D. the fuse box

5. What did Gerald's family do after dinner?
   A. finished cleaning the basement
   B. replaced the batteries in the flashlight
   C. watched home movies and looked at pictures
   D. went swimming

Meet at the Library

Before Reading

- What kinds of things can you get at a library?
- How often do you go to the library?

During Reading

- How do the boys find what they want at the library?
- What kinds of things do they read at the library?

After Reading

- Why do you think libraries are important to people?
- Which boy are you most like? Why?

Andy, Kyle, and Charles always met at the public library on Saturday. They had to return the books they'd checked out and get some new ones. They dropped them off at the counter and sat down at the computer catalogs.

Andy didn't need much time. All he ever read about was baseball. The library had everything he could ever want to know about baseball. This made Andy a big fan of the library. He disappeared into the maze of shelves to get his books.

Charles and Kyle split up and went to find what they wanted to read. Charles picked out a big book about spiders and another book about snakes. He liked creepy, crawly things. Kyle met him in the aisle. He'd already found three spy novels and two comic books, also about spies. He found a seat and started reading the comics.

Charles picked up a magazine with a big picture of a shark on the cover. He sat down beside Kyle and read about sharks. After a while, the librarian announced that the library was closing soon.

As they went to check out, Charles remembered that there were movies at the library that could be checked out. He traded his magazine for a documentary film about sharks. Kyle found two movies that he wanted to see, both with spies and long car chases. The boys checked out their items at the desk. Where was Andy? They looked all over and couldn't find him.

Finally, just as the library was closing, Andy met his friends at the front desk. He had been reading a baseball magazine. Andy checked out two books and a movie—all about baseball.

Vocabulary

maze: passage or walkway between shelves or seats
catalog: complete list of things
documentary: film that states facts about a subject
public: available to anyone

Classify/Categorize

Categorize the items read or checked out from the library by the three boys, according to which boy picked up which items.

	Andy	Kyle	Charles
Materials read at the library			
Materials checked out to take home			

#10120 Reading Comprehension—Level F *Teacher Created Materials, Inc.*

Make Inferences

Use what you read in "Meet at the Library" and what you already know to make some inferences about the story.

	What I Read	What I Know	My Inference
1. Which boy most prefers fiction to nonfiction?			
2. What can you tell about Andy's interest in baseball?			
3. Why did the boys read for a while before they looked at the movie choices?			
4. Why do you think none of the boys checked out the magazines they were reading?			

Comprehension Practice

Circle the letter of the best answer.

1. When did the boys meet at the library?
   A. every Saturday
   B. every other Saturday
   C. Sunday
   D. every day

2. Where did the boys find the library catalog?
   A. in a filing drawer
   B. in a book
   C. on a computer
   D. in a documentary film

3. What made Andy a big fan of the library?
   A. It has a good selection of spy movies.
   B. There are several magazines about sharks.
   C. It has lots of information about baseball.
   D. It is not far from his house.

4. What did Charles read about in his magazine?
   A. snakes
   B. sharks
   C. spies
   D. baseball

5. What was Andy doing when the library was closing?
   A. hiding
   B. sleeping
   C. reading a comic book
   D. reading a magazine

#10120 Reading Comprehension—Level F   *Teacher Created Materials, Inc.*

Mummies, Not Monsters

Perhaps you have seen a mummy in the movies. They are often shown as scary monsters. In reality, mummies aren't monsters at all. They are the preserved bodies of people who died long ago. Many mummies are thousands of years old.

Mummies have been found around the world. The oldest mummy in the world was found in Austria. It is thought to be more than 5,000 years old! The most famous mummies are from Egypt. Ramses II and King Tut are among the best known. These powerful rulers were buried with great treasures.

The word **mummy** comes from the Persian word **mumia**. This refers to a tarlike substance used to prepare mummies. Egyptian embalmers prepared mummies by removing moisture from the body. To do this, they used a very dry powder called natron. Today we call it baking soda. It often took over two months from the time a person died to make a mummy.

When the body was ready, it was wrapped in cloth strips. The mummy would then be placed in a series of coffins, one inside another. Wealthy people could be placed in coffins that were decorated to look like they did in life. Some people even made mummies of their pets!

Mummies are nothing to fear. They are not monsters. They are just the remains of people who lived long ago.

Before Reading

- What is a mummy?
- Have you ever seen a mummy? Where?

During Reading

- Why were people mummified?
- How were mummies prepared?

This coffin held a mummy.

After Reading

- Why do you think mummification isn't very popular today?
- Why do you think people find mummies interesting?

Vocabulary

embalmer: a person who prepares bodies for burial by making them less likely to decay

mumia: a tarlike substance used to prepare mummies

mummy: a preserved body

Use Prior Knowledge and Make Connections

Answer these questions about the selection.

1. What is the topic of the selection?

_____

2. What do you think of when you read the title? What does the title remind you of?

_____

_____

_____

_____

3. What do you think of when you look at the picture? What does the picture remind you of?

_____

_____

_____

_____

4. What did you already know about mummies? How did you learn about them?

_____

_____

_____

_____

Develop Vocabulary

Use the story content to help identify the meaning of each word. Then write your meaning and the dictionary meaning of each word.

Selection Word	What I Think the Word Means	What the Dictionary Says the Word Means
preserved		
treasure		
embalmer		
moisture		
coffin		

Comprehension Practice

Circle the letter of the best answer.

1. How are mummies often depicted?
   A. as monsters
   B. as happy people
   C. as ancient pets
   D. as giants

2. The oldest known mummy was found in _____.
   A. China
   B. America
   C. Egypt
   D. Austria

3. The most famous mummies are from _____.
   A. China
   B. Egypt
   C. America
   D. Austria

4. "Natron" is another word for what?
   A. chalk
   B. dust
   C. baking soda
   D. flour

5. How long did the mummification process take?
   A. two hours
   B. 20 hours
   C. two weeks
   D. over two months

The Mighty Mineral

Rocks are made of minerals. But what are minerals? They are solid, natural substances made of basic elements like carbon and calcium. Minerals are found everywhere, even in our food. Spinach and sunflower seeds are rich in iron. Nuts contain copper and zinc. Table salt is really a mineral called halite. Toothpaste has a form of fluorite to help prevent cavities.

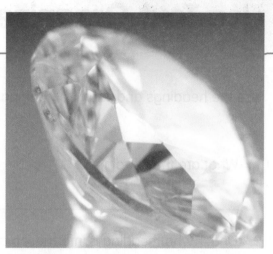

Diamond

Metals and Gems

Metals like lead, silver, and gold are minerals. So are gems such as diamonds, rubies, and emeralds.

Crystals

Many minerals take the form of crystals. They can look like cubes or other shapes. In some rocks, you can see the tiny mineral crystals that make up the rock. Granite is such a rock.

Hardness

Minerals have different shapes, colors, weights, and degrees of hardness. In 1812, Friedrich Mohs created a scale to tell the hardness of each mineral. The Mohs hardness scale ranges from 1 to 10. Talc, used to make some kinds of powder, is the softest. It rates only 1 on the Mohs scale. The graphite we use in pencil leads is very soft. It rates between 1 and 2. Corundum, found in rubies and sapphires, is very hard. It rates a 9 on the scale. Diamond, the world's hardest mineral, rates a 10.

Mohs Hardness Scale	
Hardness	**Mineral**
1	talc
2	gypsum
3	calcite
4	fluorite
5	apatite
6	feldspar
7	quartz
8	topaz
9	corundum
10	diamond

Before Reading

- What are rocks made of?
- What are some minerals?

During Reading

- Where do we find minerals?
- Which minerals are hard? Which ones are soft?

After Reading

- How are minerals good for our bodies?
- In what other ways do we use minerals?

Vocabulary

mineral: a natural material found in the earth that is neither a plant nor an animal

elements: the simplest type of natural substance, from which all other things are made

crystals: regularly shaped pieces with flat surfaces and many angles, which can come in many shapes

Use Text Organizers

Use the headings and chart from the passage to answer these questions.

1. What are the headings?

   _____

2. Under what heading is information about gold?

   _____

3. What information is given under the heading "Hardness"?

   _____

4. What information does the chart provide?

   _____

   _____

   _____

5. What minerals can scratch quartz?

   _____

6. Why can't talc scratch any minerals?

   _____

7. What mineral can a diamond scratch? Explain.

   _____

8. A fingernail can scratch talc. What does this tell you about the hardness of a fingernail?

   _____

Identify Main Idea and Supporting Details

The top chart shows the main idea and supporting details for the first paragraph of the selection. Fill in the bottom chart for the last paragraph of the selection.

Topic: Minerals
Main Idea: Minerals are useful substances found in many places.
Detail: Spinach and sunflower seeds contain iron.
Detail: Nuts contain zinc and copper.
Detail: Table salt is made of the mineral halite.
Detail: Fluorite is used to make toothpaste.

Topic:
Main Idea:
Detail:
Detail:
Detail:
Detail:
Detail:

Comprehension Practice

Circle the letter of the best answer.

1. What are all rocks made of?
   A. granite
   B. sand
   C. calcium
   D. minerals

2. What is another name for table salt?
   A. saccharine
   B. sodium
   C. halite
   D. calcium

3. Which of the following is a good source of iron?
   A. granite
   B. nuts
   C. spinach
   D. table salt

4. What does the Mohs scale tell about minerals?
   A. weight
   B. hardness
   C. crystal shape
   D. color

5. What is the hardest mineral?
   A. talc
   B. graphite
   C. corundum
   D. diamond

Giving It All Away

Chris and Molly ran into the house just as it started to storm. Their mom saw on the news that it was supposed to rain all day. So she asked the two kids to gather up all the clothes that no longer fit and put them in a box. Tomorrow, they would donate the clothes to charity.

Chris and Molly wondered why they didn't just have a yard sale and sell all their old stuff. Their mom explained that it was good to donate. She said that the thrift stores sell the contributions and use the money they make to help needy people.

Chris went through his dresser, pulling out all the jeans, shorts, and shirts that he had outgrown. Then he started on his closet. A few sweaters, some dress pants and dress shirts, a jacket, and some shoes all went into the give-away box.

Molly pulled out a dress, some pants, several sweaters, and some shirts, all of which were too small for her. She even found a hat she had forgotten about.

The kids discovered it was fun to think about what to give away. They started going through their old toys, books, games, dolls, and stuffed animals. They pulled out everything they didn't use anymore.

When they finished, Chris and Molly had enough things to fill up three boxes! While their mom helped them pack it all up, the kids felt good because they knew they were helping people.

Before Reading

- What does your family do with things you no longer need?
- What kinds of things do you find at a thrift store?

During Reading

- Where does the story take place?
- What kinds of things do the kids donate?

After Reading

- Were you surprised that the kids wanted to donate so much? Why or why not?
- Why do you think people like to help others?

Vocabulary

contribution: something given as a gift

donate: to give away

thrift: careful use of money

Ask Questions

As you read the story, you may have asked yourself questions like the ones below. Look for answers to the questions in the article. Write the answers on the lines.

1. Why are the children packing up their old clothes?

   _____

   _____

2. What is a charity?

   _____

   _____

3. What is a thrift store?

   _____

   _____

4. What do thrift stores do with their profits?

   _____

   _____

5. What kinds of things do the children give to the thrift shop?

   _____

   _____

6. How were the children helping other people?

   _____

   _____

Identify Author's Purpose and Viewpoint

1. What reasons might the author have had for writing "Giving It All Away"?

_____

_____

_____

_____

_____

_____

_____

_____

_____

2. Why does the author think thrift shops are good places?

_____

_____

_____

_____

_____

_____

_____

_____

_____

_____

Comprehension Practice

Circle the letter of the best answer.

1. What does Mom learn from the news show?
   A. Snow is coming.
   B. It is going to rain all day.
   C. A new thrift shop is opening.
   D. There are many people in need.

2. What did the kids first think of doing with their extra things?
   A. donate them
   B. throw them away
   C. sell them at a yard sale
   D. keep them

3. What did the kids NOT put in the box?
   A. clothes
   B. toys
   C. books
   D. food

4. What does a thrift shop do?
   A. sell donated items to raise money to help people
   B. prepare weather reports for news programs
   C. sell boxes that people can use to collect donations
   D. teach children about saving their money

5. How many boxes did the kids fill?
   A. one
   B. two
   C. three
   D. four

A Whale of a Shark

Of all the creatures on Earth, sharks are long-time residents. Sharks have lived here since well before the dinosaurs roamed the land. Today, they live in every ocean and even in some rivers and lakes.

Sharks are flexible fish. Unlike bony fish, sharks have no bones. Their skeletons are made of cartilage.

The largest of all the sharks is the whale shark. Whale sharks can grow up to 40 feet, or 12 meters, long and may live 100 to 150 years. They have distinctive yellow stripes and dots on their gray skin.

Whale sharks have about 3,000 small teeth in their large mouths. But they don't use their teeth for chewing. These huge animals are filter feeders.

A whale shark swims with its huge mouth open. It takes in lots of water filled with small sea creatures. The water is filtered through the shark's gills. The whale shark eats anything that doesn't pass through the gills, including plankton, small fish, and squid. Up to 1,500 gallons, or 5,678 liters, of water can pass through a whale shark's gills each hour!

Whale sharks are wanderers, although they swim slowly at about 3 miles, or 4.8 kilometers, per hour. To swim, whale sharks must move their entire bodies from side to side. They tend to travel alone. They live in the warmer ocean waters and travel in both open and coastal waters.

Before Reading

- What are sharks?
- Where are sharks found?

During Reading

- How are sharks different from bony fish?
- How and what do whale sharks eat?

Whale Shark

After Reading

- Why is "whale shark" a good name for the largest shark?
- Why do you think sharks have been able to survive so long on Earth?

Vocabulary

whale shark: the largest of all sharks

cartilage: an elastic connective material that isn't as hard as bone

filter feeder: an animal that eats material that does not pass through gills

Develop Vocabulary

Use the story content to help identify the meaning of each word. Then write your meaning and the dictionary meaning of each word.

Selection Word	What I Think the Word Means	What the Dictionary Says the Word Means
resident		
flexible		
distinctive		
plankton		
wanderer		

Identify Main Idea and Supporting Details

Complete the chart by identifying the main idea and supporting details of each paragraph.

Paragraph	Main Idea	Supporting Details
1		
2		
3		
4		
5		
6		

Comprehension Practice

Circle the letter of the best answer.

1. How many bones does a whale shark have?
   A. 4
   B. 150
   C. 3000
   D. none

2. How many years might a whale shark live?
   A. 20
   B. 40–60
   C. 100–150
   D. 200–225

3. What kinds of markings does a whale shark have?
   A. gray and white stripes
   B. brown and orange lines
   C. yellowish dots and stripes
   D. gray and white spots

4. How does a whale shark eat?
   A. It dives for fish.
   B. It filters food from water.
   C. It sneaks up on prey.
   D. It hunts and opens shell fish.

5. Where do whale sharks live?
   A. Arctic Ocean
   B. icy lakes and rivers
   C. Antarctica
   D. warm oceans

A Day at the Art Museum

Last week, Mr. Grizzle's class went on a field trip to an art museum. Mr. Grizzle told the class that the museum was one of the biggest in the world. A person could spend a whole week there and still not see all the great displays.

They first went into a huge area that had many kinds of art from North America. Some paintings showed scenes from colonial times. Others were more recent paintings. Sometimes it was hard to tell what some of the pictures were! Other rooms had giant photos of people, rooms, and cities. Sculptures were scattered around. In a separate room, the class saw dolls, beads, moccasins, and clothes made hundreds of years ago by Native Americans.

In the Asian area, the class saw the same kinds of newer paintings, photos, and sculptures. But they also saw very different kinds of art. There were many suits of armor and a huge collection of swords and shields. There were also relics from thousands of years ago. Sculptures, clothes, dolls, and many things carved from stone were on display in the Asian room.

Other rooms featured African and European art. Art from so many cultures could be seen here! At the end of the day, Mr. Grizzle's students begged to come back. Coming to the museum was like taking a trip around the world.

Before Reading

- What is a museum?
- What kinds of museums have you been to?

During Reading

- Where does a museum get its art?
- What different types of art did the class see?

Moccasins

After Reading

- Why do you think people are fascinated by ancient art?
- Why do you think art museums are important?

Vocabulary

moccasin: a soft leather shoe with no sole or heel

museum: a place where art and historical artifacts are displayed and studied

relic: an object remaining after decay or disappearance

Compare and Contrast

Use the diagram below to compare the types of museum items that came from North America and from Asia. In the circle on the left, write names of items that came from North America. In the circle on the right, write names of items that came from Asia. In the area where the two circles overlap, write names of items from both continents.

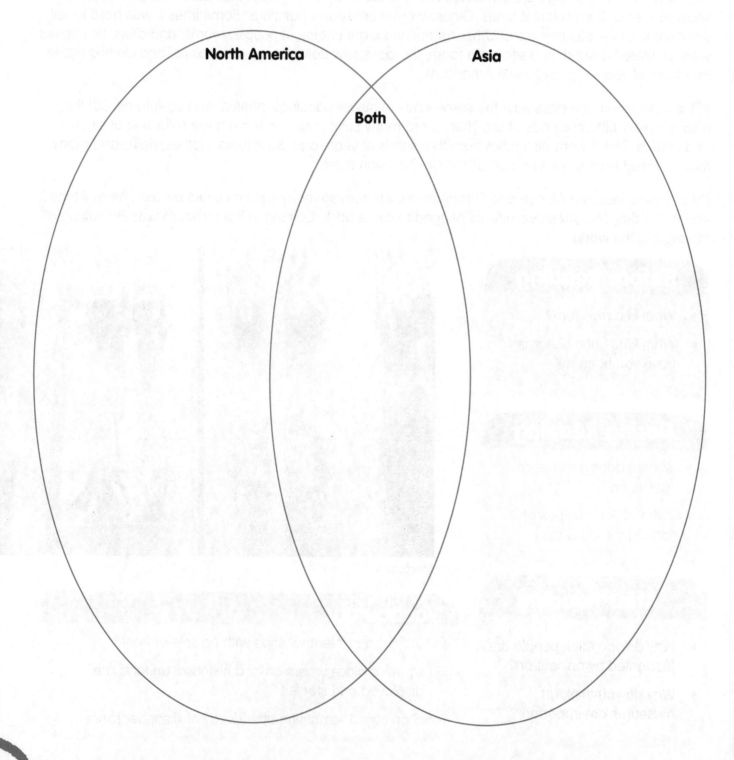

North America

Both

Asia

Visualize

Visualize one of the areas the students visited at the art museum. Picture this scene in your mind and draw what you see. Then describe it on the lines below.

Comprehension Practice

Circle the letter of the best answer.

1. Who did Mr. Grizzle take to the art museum?
   A. his kids
   B. his wife
   C. his students
   D. his friends

2. What was not on display in the North America art room?
   A. paintings
   B. photos
   C. clothing
   D. dishes

3. Who made the moccasins?
   A. Asians
   B. Native Americans
   C. modern artists
   D. museum visitors

4. What was not on display in the Asian room?
   A. stone carvings
   B. armor
   C. beads
   D. paintings

5. At the end of the story, what did the class want to do?
   A. go home
   B. go back to school
   C. go to another museum
   D. come back to the art museum

The Great Apes

Have you ever seen a gorilla, chimpanzee, or orangutan? You might think that these animals, known as great apes, look like large monkeys. But are they? The answer is no. Great apes are bigger and have fewer babies than monkeys. They also stand upright more, and they depend more on their eyes than on their noses. Apes don't have tails like monkeys do. The most important distinction is all in their heads. Apes' brains are larger and more developed, which means they're smarter than monkeys.

Great apes have prehensile feet. That means they are able to grab things. Apes have

Chimpanzee

unique fingerprints and flat fingernails. The ape's body is designed to walk on all fours. Apes' arms are longer than their legs, so they use their knuckles to walk.

Apes have gestures and make faces that look almost human. However, they can mean very different things to apes than they do to people. For example, what looks like a big smile on a chimpanzee's face may really be a "fear grin" that means the chimp is afraid.

The great apes may remind you of monkeys. They may make humanlike faces. However, they are their own kind of animal. They have their own characteristics that make them unique.

Vocabulary

distinction: a difference

gestures: movements to help express an idea or emotion

prehensile: able to grab things

Ask Questions

As you read the story, you may have asked yourself questions like the ones below. Look for answers to the questions in the article. Write the answers on the lines.

1. Name three great apes.

    _____

    _____

2. Why do apes use their knuckles when walking on all fours?

    _____

    _____

3. In what ways do apes look almost human?

    _____

    _____

4. How are apes different from monkeys?

    _____

    _____

5. Why can apes grab things?

    _____

    _____

6. Could you identify an ape from its fingerprints? Explain.

    _____

    _____

Identify Main Idea and Supporting Details

The chart shows the main ideas for the selection. Write details from the text that support each main idea.

Paragraph 1 Topic: Great Apes
Paragraph 1 Main Idea: Great apes are different from monkeys.
Detail:
Detail:
Detail:
Detail:
Detail:
Detail:
Paragraphs 2 and 3 Topic: Physical Characteristics of Apes
Paragraphs 2 and 3 Main Idea: The great apes have certain physical characteristics that set them apart.
Detail:
Detail:
Detail:
Detail:
Detail:

Comprehension Practice

Circle the letter of the best answer.

1. What do great apes depend on more than monkeys do?
   A. ears
   B. tails
   C. noses
   D. eyes

2. Which of these has a tail?
   A. orangutan
   B. monkey
   C. chimpanzee
   D. gorilla

3. Why are great apes able to grasp things with their feet?
   A. They have fingerprints on their feet.
   B. They pick things up with their fingernails.
   C. Their feet are prehensile.
   D. They use two feet at a time to pick things up.

4. What is one thing that humans have that great apes also have?
   A. tails
   B. longer arms than legs
   C. fingerprints
   D. jeans

5. What might a frightened chimpanzee do?
   A. cover its ears
   B. wave
   C. sit down
   D. smile

About Belugas

Beluga whales are "white whales," but they're not born white. Calves are brownish-gray. They get lighter and lighter until they become completely white by the time they are six years old.

Belugas always seem to be smiling. Maybe this is why they are so popular at zoos and aquariums.

Unlike other whales, belugas can turn their heads and make faces. Also, belugas don't migrate from place to place as many other whales do. Belugas spend their lives in the cold Arctic Circle. How do they stay warm? Belugas have a layer of blubber, or fat, to keep them warm.

Belugas, like most whales, have good hearing and vision. Unlike most other whales, belugas do not have a dorsal fin. A dorsal fin is a fin at the back and on the top of some whales and fish, including sharks. In fact, the Latin name for beluga means "dolphin-without-a-wing."

In the nineteenth century, sailors called belugas "sea canaries." The belugas sing to one another. They make clicking and chirping sounds. A pod, or group, of belugas can be very noisy! Belugas can bounce sounds off things under the water to see how far away they are. This helps the whales locate food sources.

Before Reading

- What are belugas?
- What do belugas look like?

During Reading

- What are some other names for belugas?
- How do belugas use sound?

After Reading

- Why do you think people like belugas so much?
- How are belugas different from other whales?

Vocabulary

Arctic Circle: the region surrounding the North Pole

dorsal fin: a winglike part near the back of a whale or fish

migrate: to move from one region to another

pod: a group of whales

Use Prior Knowledge and Make Connections

Answer these questions about the selection.

1. What is the topic of the selection?

   _____

2. What do you think of when you read the title? What does the title remind you of?

   _____

   _____

   _____

   _____

3. What do you think of when you look at the picture? What does the picture remind you of?

   _____

   _____

   _____

   _____

4. Have you had any experience with the topic? If so, what was your experience?

   _____

   _____

   _____

   _____

Develop Vocabulary

Use the story content to help identify the meaning of each word. Then write your meaning and the dictionary meaning of each word.

Selection Word	What I Think the Word Means	What the Dictionary Says the Word Means
whale		
aquarium		
calf		
pod		
dorsal fin		

Comprehension Practice

Circle the letter of the best answer.

1. What color is a baby beluga?
   A. white
   B. brown
   C. brownish gray
   D. bluish white

2. What is a baby beluga called?
   A. cub
   B. calf
   C. tadpole
   D. fish

3. What keeps belugas warm?
   A. water
   B. blubber
   C. weather
   D. swimming fast

4. What do many other whales have that belugas do not have?
   A. good hearing
   B. dorsal fins
   C. good vision
   D. pods

5. What did sailors nickname belugas?
   A. white whales
   B. dolphins without wings
   C. water wonders
   D. sea canaries

Bettina and the Mukluk Song

Ages ago, in a kingdom far away, there lived a girl named Bettina. She lived with her poor father at the foot of a great mountain. Bettina always sang lovely songs to keep her father happy. However, she had to be careful not to be heard by anyone but her father, for the Mukluk was bound to come if he heard. The Mukluk was a creature of the mountain who wanted to steal all music and make the world gloomy.

One day, Bettina was singing her tune softly and pulling a cart of coal to their hovel. Suddenly, Bettina heard a great banging and clanging. She was sure it was the Mukluk and that he had heard her song. Bravely, she sang louder and louder to show him she was not afraid. In time, the clanging stopped.

This went on for many days. Bettina hummed her song and did her chores. The banging would come and Bettina would sing her lovely song louder until the noise stopped.

One day, there was no banging or clanging. As Bettina hummed softly, she saw a pretty butterfly outside the window. She sang her tune to the butterfly until it fluttered away.

The following day, the butterfly came again. This time, it brought with it a handsome prince! The prince explained that he had been the Mukluk. He had come to steal her music, but instead he had been soothed by her song. The spell that had made him the gloomy Mukluk was broken by her brave and beautiful song!

Bettina and her father went to live in the prince's castle. There she sang her lovely songs all day and made every heart glad.

Vocabulary

hovel: a small, dirty shelter

kingdom: a place ruled by a king or queen

soothed: calmed

Before Reading

- What is a fairy tale?
- What fairy tales do you know?

During Reading

- Where and when does the story take place?
- Will the Mukluk capture Bettina?

After Reading

- Were you surprised by the prince? Why or why not?
- How is this story unlike a real-life story?

Predict

Before and during reading, use your own knowledge and imagination to predict what is going to happen next in the story.

1. Read the first paragraph, then stop. Write down what you think will happen to Bettina and her father. Why do you think so?

   _____

   _____

   _____

2. Read the fourth paragraph of the story, then stop. Write your prediction about what is going to happen with the butterfly.

   _____

   _____

   _____

3. When you finish reading, check your predictions. How do your predictions compare to the story? Are your predictions more or less realistic than the story?

   _____

   _____

   _____

4. Write an ending to the story. Predict what Bettina will do. Will Bettina and her father stay at the castle? Will Bettina marry and have children who sing?

   _____

   _____

   _____

Identify Story Elements

Summarize the different elements of "Bettina and the Mukluk Song" in the chart.

Bettina and the Mukluk Song	
Setting: When and where did the story happen?	
Characters: Who are the characters? What did you learn about them?	
Plot: What is the important action of the story?	

Comprehension Practice

Circle the letter of the best answer.

1. What did the Mukluk want to steal?
   A. beauty
   B. music
   C. coal
   D. color

2. What did Bettina do to show the Mukluk she was not afraid?
   A. shouted at it
   B. threw coal at it
   C. sang loudly
   D. hummed softly

3. How many times did the Mukluk come to the mountain?
   A. once
   B. twice
   C. several times
   D. for many days

4. Who did the Mukluk turn out to be?
   A. a magical butterfly
   B. Bettina's father
   C. a prince
   D. a queen

5. What happened to Bettina?
   A. She was put in a zoo.
   B. She went to live at the castle.
   C. She became a traveling musician.
   D. She married the prince.

    Teacher Created Materials, Inc.

The Story of Chewing Gum

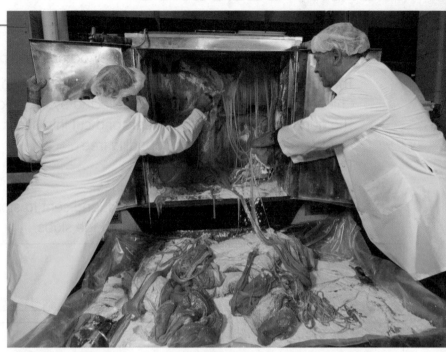
Workers in a factory making bubble gum.

Chewing gum was discovered a thousand years ago by Mayans in the Mexican jungles. They found a liquid leaking from a sapodilla tree. The liquid was sweet. As it oozed out, it thickened into something that they called chicle (CHEEK lay). The Mayans found that this chewable chicle was quite tasty.

Today, workers called chicleros still collect chicle. A chiclero cuts the bark of a tree. He or she lets the liquid run into buckets. He or she has to cut the tree just right so that it isn't hurt. The chicle is boiled to remove the water. It is then made into slabs about 30 pounds, or 14 kilograms, each. These slabs are then sent to gum factories.

At a gum factory, machines take over most of the work. The chicle is placed in big kettles for cleaning. The cleaned chicle is then moved into other kettles. There it is mixed with ingredients to sweeten, soften, flavor, and color the gum.

After the gum is mixed and cooled, it is pressed into wide, flat sheets. Some machines divide the gum into smaller sheets. Other machines cut the sheets into single sticks of gum. Finally, the sticks of gum are wrapped in foil and paper. Now they're ready for the next gum-chewing customer that comes along!

Before Reading

- What does the word "gum" mean?
- What do you think chewing gum is made of?

During Reading

- What things do people do in the gum-making process?
- What do machines do in the process?

After Reading

- Where do you think gum goes after it is packaged?
- What are some other products made from trees?

Vocabulary

chicle: the main ingredient in chewing gum

chiclero: a person who extracts chicle from a sapodilla tree

oozed: leaked or dripped slowly

sapodilla: a type of tree with sap that turns into chewable chicle

Identify Sequence

Write the steps below in the order in which they occur in the process of making chewing gum.

The chicle is mixed with ingredients to sweeten, soften, and flavor it.

Chicle oozes out of the tree and is collected by the chicleros.

The gum is pressed into thin sheets and cut into sticks.

A chiclero cuts the bark of a sapodilla tree.

The chicle is cleaned at a factory.

Slabs of chicle are sent to gum factories.

Sticks of gum are wrapped, packaged, and sent to stores.

Chicle is boiled and then molded into huge slabs.

1.

2.

3.

4.

5.

6.

7.

8.

Identify Main Idea and Supporting Details

The top chart shows the main idea and supporting details for the first two paragraphs of the selection. Fill in the bottom chart for the last two paragraphs of the selection.

Topic: Chicle
Main Idea: Chicle was discovered in Mexico and is still harvested.
Detail: Chicle was discovered by the Mayans 1,000 years ago.
Detail: Chicle is thickened sap from a sapodilla tree.
Detail: Chicle is sweet and chewable.
Detail: Workers called chicleros collect chicle for gum makers.
Detail: They cut the trees, collect the sap, boil it, and make it into slabs.

Topic:
Main Idea:
Detail:
Detail:
Detail:
Detail:
Detail:

Comprehension Practice

Circle the letter of the best answer.

1. Who "discovered" chewing gum?
   A. Mayans
   B. sapodillas
   C. chicleros
   D. gum factories

2. What is a name for workers who collect chicle?
   A. sapodillas
   B. Mayans
   C. chicleros
   D. gummers

3. Why does the chiclero have to be careful when cutting the tree?
   A. to make sure he or she doesn't fall
   B. to make sure the tree doesn't get hurt
   C. to make sure no chicle is left behind
   D. to make sure the chicle does not ooze out of the tree

4. Where are the slabs of chicle sent?
   A. to recycling centers
   B. to gum factories
   C. to the Mexican jungle
   D. to candy stores

5. Ingredients are added to chicle to do all of the following EXCEPT _____.
   A. soften it
   B. flavor it
   C. make it chewable
   D. make it sweeter

Penguin or . . . Puffin?

Before Reading

- What is a puffin?
- What is a penguin?

During Reading

- How is a puffin like a penguin?
- How is a puffin different from a penguin?

After Reading

- Why might people confuse puffins and penguins?
- Would penguins and puffins be likely to compete for food? Why or why not?

People have been confusing penguins and puffins for years. After all, both are black-and-white sea birds. Both birds are very good swimmers. Both live in cold climates. However, penguins live in the icy south while puffins live in the Northern Hemisphere. And, unlike the flightless penguin, puffins can fly.

Penguins are larger than puffins. Some penguins are about 15 inches, or 0.4 meters, tall. Others are almost 4 feet, or 1.2 meters, tall. The largest puffin is only about 12 inches, or 0.3 meters, tall.

The penguin has a thin beak. It can be black, purple, red, or orange. The puffin's beak looks like a triangle. This oddly-shaped beak may be orange, yellow, blue, or red. Because of their beaks, puffins have been called "sea parrots" and "clowns of the sea."

Puffin

Both birds can dive, but penguins are the better divers. Some can dive about 800 feet, or 244 meters. Puffins can dive only about 80 feet, or 24 meters. Both birds have layers of fat that help keep them warm. Their feathers are also waterproof.

In the water, the black-and-white bodies of penguins and puffins help them hide from enemies. As seen from below, the belly blends in with the color of the seawater. From above, the dark back is the color of the dark sea floor.

There's no need to be confused. The birds are alike in some ways, but they are also very different.

Vocabulary

climate: the usual weather in a place
flightless: unable to fly
waterproof: able to keep water off

Penguin

Compare and Contrast

Use this Venn diagram to tell how penguins and puffins are alike and different.

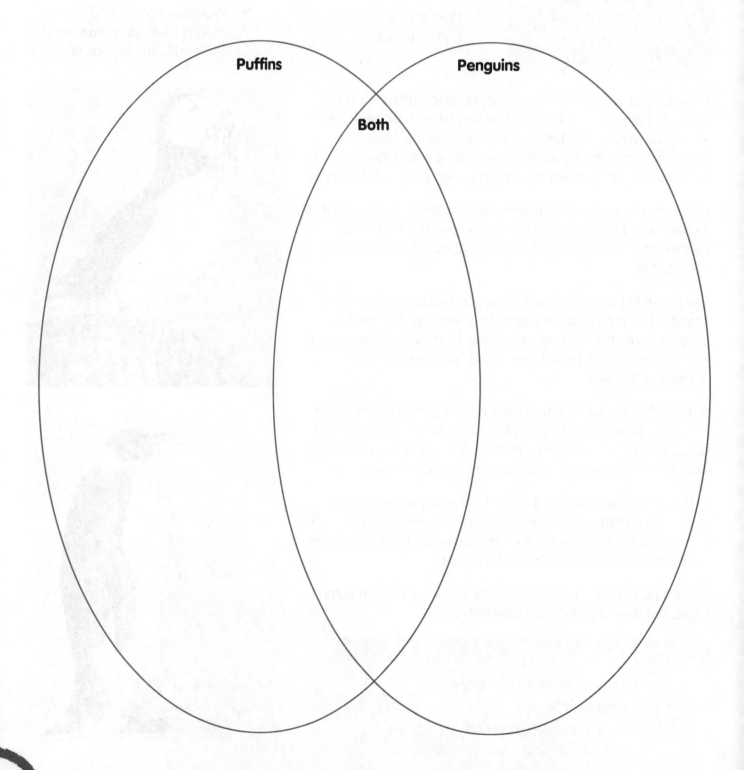

Puffins

Penguins

Both

Summarize and Paraphrase

Summarize each paragraph of the selection in your own words. Be sure to include the main idea and important details in your summary.

Paragraph 1:

_____

_____

_____

Paragraph 2:

_____

_____

_____

Paragraph 3:

_____

_____

_____

Paragraph 4:

_____

_____

_____

Paragraph 5:

_____

_____

_____

Comprehension Practice

Circle the letter of the best answer.

1. Where do puffins live?
   A. Antarctica
   B. south
   C. Northern Hemisphere
   D. Africa

2. What feature distinguishes a puffin from a penguin?
   A. ability to fly
   B. living in a cold climate
   C. black-and-white body
   D. ability to swim

3. How are puffins and penguins alike?
   A. shape of their beaks
   B. size
   C. where they live
   D. color of bodies

4. How much deeper than puffins can some penguins dive?
   A. 1 mile, or 1.6 kilometers
   B. 8 feet, or 2.4 meters
   C. 1,000 feet, or 305 meters
   D. 720 feet, or 220 meters

5. What helps keep puffins and penguins warm?
   A. layers of fat
   B. flapping wings
   C. white feathers
   D. perching under rocks

Lara's Lesson

One day, Tony walked home from the park where he had baseball practice. His sister Lara was home from college, and he was excited to show off his baseball uniform.

As he approached his house, Tony saw Lara's car parked in the driveway and hurried. He decided to go around to the back door to surprise his sister.

When he got to the door, he noticed a yellow sticky note on the door. On the sticky note was a word he didn't know. Tony shrugged and opened the door.

Inside the kitchen, Tony observed that everything had a tiny sticky note on it—the sink, table, chairs, refrigerator, oven, and microwave. Even the flowers had a sticky note on them! Each note had a different word on it. He raised his eyebrows and went into the family room to find his sister.

Again, he found tiny sticky notes everywhere. The couch, recliner, TV, stereo, and bookshelves were all labeled with strange words. And where was Lara?

He went up the sticky yellow-labeled staircase to his room. Just as Tony had suspected, his room was plastered with notes. His bed, lamp, closet, and desk all wore sticky notes. Even his baseball bat had a note on it! What was going on?

"Hey, kiddo," he heard his sister say. Tony turned around as Lara was putting a sticky note on his light switch.

"What are you doing?" Tony asked. Lara explained to Tony that the words were Spanish for the things they were stuck on. The notes were helping Lara learn Spanish!

Before Reading

- What have you used sticky notes for?
- What are some words you know from another language?

During Reading

- What happens when Tony enters the house?
- Where does Lara put sticky notes?

After Reading

- Were you surprised at what Lara was doing? Why or why not?
- Why do you think people learn different languages?

Vocabulary

approached: got closer to

plastered: covered

suspected: thought something was likely

Classify/Categorize

Summarize the different elements of "Lara's Lesson" in the chart.

Kitchen	Family Room	Bedroom

Make Inferences

Use what you read in "Lara's Lesson" and what you know to make some inferences about the story.

		What I Read	What I Know	My Inference
1.	Where was Tony's baseball uniform?			
2.	Whose car is parked in the driveway?			
3.	Where was Lara while Tony was looking around at the notes in the house?			
4.	How will the notes help Lara learn Spanish?			

Comprehension Practice

Circle the letter of the best answer.

1. What did Tony want to show his sister?
   A. his new uniform
   B. his baseball glove
   C. his baseball bat
   D. an autographed baseball

2. Why didn't Tony use the front door?
   A. It was locked.
   B. It had a note on it.
   C. Lara was using it.
   D. He wanted to surprise Lara.

3. What did NOT have a sticky note on it when Tony first got home?
   A. flowers in the kitchen
   B. his bedroom light switch
   C. the stereo
   D. the couch

4. What did Tony think he would find in his room?
   A. Lara
   B. his baseball bat
   C. yellow sticky notes
   D. his parents

5. What was written on the sticky notes?
   A. made-up words
   B. funny poems
   C. reminders about Tony's chores
   D. Spanish words

The Great Pyramids

Before Reading

- What does a pyramid look like?
- What do you know about pyramids?

During Reading

- When were pyramids built?
- Why were pyramids built?

After Reading

- How do you think the pyramids have lasted so long?
- How do you think people built the pyramids?

The pyramids of Egypt are some of the most amazing buildings on Earth. A pyramid is a large building with a square base. It has four sloping, triangular sides. They come to a point at the top. The pyramids were made of huge blocks of stone. These stones were laid so perfectly that not even a tiny space was left. A pyramid took thousands of workers and many years to complete.

Egyptians used the great pyramids as tombs for pharaohs, or kings. The most famous ones were built about 4,500 years ago. Egyptians thought a person lived forever. They mummified, or dried and preserved, the kings' bodies. Then they buried them in these great tombs. They put treasures and food in the tombs for use in the next life.

Many large pyramids were surrounded by smaller ones. These were used for the king's wife and children. The king's officials were also buried nearby in small tombs. These tombs, called mastabas, had sloping sides and flat roofs.

The ruins of 35 major pyramids and 40 small ones still stand near the Nile River. The largest is the Great Pyramid of Khufu. It was 481 feet, or 146 meters, tall when built. It was Earth's tallest building for more than 4,000 years!

These huge buildings provide clues to ancient times. They also serve as a reminder of Egypt's great past.

Pyramids of Khufu

Vocabulary

mastabas: small Egyptian tombs built for the king's officials

mummified: prepared as a mummy by drying the body and wrapping it in cloth

pyramid: a structure with a square base and sloping, triangular sides

Identify Main Idea and Supporting Details

The top chart shows the main idea and supporting details for the first paragraph of the selection. Fill in the bottom chart for the second paragraph of the selection.

Topic: Pyramids
Main Idea: A pyramid is a specially-shaped building.
Detail: A pyramid is large, with a square base.
Detail: A pyramid has four triangular sides.
Detail: A pyramid comes to a point at the top.
Detail: A pyramid is made of large stone blocks.

Topic:
Main Idea:
Detail:
Detail:
Detail:
Detail:

Identify Author's Purpose and Viewpoint

Authors write for many different reasons. Think about why the author wrote "The Great Pyramids." Then answer the questions.

1. What is the subject of the story?

   _____

2. Does this story tell facts about the subject?

   _____

   If so, write three facts given in the article.

   _____

   _____

   _____

3. Does this story mostly entertain?

   _____

4. Does the story try to persuade you to do something?

   _____

5. Does the story try to persuade you to believe something?

   _____

6. Think about your answers to questions 1–5. Then circle the reason why the author wrote the article. Explain on the lines below.

   to entertain   to inform   to persuade

   _____

   _____

   _____

Comprehension Practice

Circle the letter of the best answer.

1. How old are the great pyramids?
   A. 2,000 years
   B. 3,000 years
   C. 4,500 years
   D. No one knows.

2. What were ancient Egyptian kings called?
   A. mummies
   B. pharaohs
   C. officials
   D. mastabas

3. Pyramids were used as _____.
   A. houses
   B. tombs
   C. funeral parlors
   D. hiding places

4. How many major pyramids still stand?
   A. 3
   B. 13
   C. 35
   D. none

5. Who was buried in the mastabas?
   A. queens
   B. officials
   C. pharaohs
   D. servants

Uncle Ed's Store

Before Reading

- What are sporting goods?
- What kinds of jobs might a person do in a store?

During Reading

- What are Daniel's jobs at the store?
- What kinds of things does the store sell?

After Reading

- Why do you think Uncle Ed wants everything in order?
- Would you have laughed about the tennis balls? Why or why not?

Every other Sunday, Daniel helps Uncle Ed at his sporting goods store. He helps clean up the floor, tidy the clothing racks, and make sure the shelves are all arranged nicely.

First, Daniel makes sure there is nothing on the floor. Uncle Ed gives him boxes of new clothes to hang on the proper racks. There are running suits, shorts, swimsuits, tee shirts, golf shirts, and tennis dresses. All these different things hang in their own places. Daniel arranges them by size and moves on to the shoes.

Uncle Ed leaves big boxes of shoes out for Daniel to put in order on the shelves. He arranges them by brand, color, and size. There are running shoes, tennis shoes, and golf shoes in the middle. Baseball and football shoes go on the left, hiking boots on the bottom. Basketball and skateboard shoes go up on the top.

After he takes out the trash, Daniel sorts the golf clubs, skiing gear, and baseball mitts. His last job is to arrange the different types of balls. Baseballs go in a big basket in the corner. Golf balls sit on a shelf in little boxes. Softballs, rubber balls, and basketballs also sit on shelves. But some of them get loaded into huge cages that almost touch the ceiling.

One time, Uncle Ed filled one of the big cages with tennis balls. By accident, Daniel opened the door at the bottom of the cages and all the tennis balls spilled out onto the floor. Tennis balls bounced all over the store! He and his uncle still laugh about it sometimes.

Vocabulary

accident: something that a person does without meaning to

arrange: put in a certain order

Classify/Categorize

List the various items that Daniel puts away in the store under each category below.

Clothes	Shoes	Equipment

Identify Sequence

Write the jobs below in the order in which Daniel does them.

arranges different kinds of balls

puts shoes in order on shelves

takes out trash

arranges new clothes on racks

cleans up floor

sorts golf clubs, skiing gear, and baseball mitts

1.

2.

3.

4.

5.

6.

Comprehension Practice

Circle the letter of the best answer.

1. What job does Daniel NOT do at the store?
   A. help customers
   B. arrange shoes
   C. hang clothes
   D. arrange golf clubs

2. How does Daniel arrange the clothes?
   A. by color
   B. by brand
   C. by size
   D. by sleeve length

3. Uncle Ed's store sells all of the following kinds of shoes EXCEPT _____.
   A. tennis shoes
   B. hiking boots
   C. football shoes
   D. bowling shoes

4. Which kind of ball goes in a basket?
   A. golf ball
   B. baseball
   C. softball
   D. rubber ball

5. What did Daniel once spill on the floor?
   A. rubber balls
   B. a box of new shoes
   C. tennis balls
   D. golf clubs

     Teacher Created Materials, Inc.

Plenty About Pandas

The rare giant panda is a small bear. Its head is white, with black ears and black "patches" around its eyes. Pandas can weigh up to 275 pounds (125 kilograms). They live mostly on bamboo. They can eat up to 33 pounds (15 kilograms) of bamboo every day! In addition, pandas have unusual paws. Their wrist bone can be used like a human thumb.

Long ago, people thought pandas had magical powers. They were even kept as pets by kings. However, their stately history hasn't kept them safe. Giant pandas are in danger. Humans have moved into the forests where they live. They have cut down the trees pandas need to survive. Now only a few places in China have enough bamboo for pandas. There are only about 1,600 giant pandas living in the Chinese forests now.

People have been trying to keep pandas safe in zoos. Unfortunately, pandas don't breed well in captivity. This means that the pandas that come into zoos may be safe from harm, but they don't have enough babies to increase the number of pandas.

China and other countries are working hard to save pandas. Some forest areas are now protected. Some zoos are studying how to help pandas breed. They want to make sure these animals are around for a long time to come.

Before Reading

- Have you ever seen a panda? Where?

- What do you know about pandas?

During Reading

- Where do pandas live?

- How are pandas different from other bears?

After Reading

- Why do you think people like pandas so much?

- How can people help pandas?

Vocabulary

bamboo: woody grasses found in China and Southeast Asia

breed: to reproduce

captivity: the state of being secured in a place, such as in a zoo

rare: not common; not easily found

Make Inferences

Use what you read in "Plenty About Pandas" and what you already know to make some inferences.

		What I Read	What I Know	My Inference
1.	Why do you think pandas have become so rare?			
2.	Why did kings once keep pandas as royal pets?			
3.	What specific things can people do to help pandas?			
4.	What difficulties do animals have in captivity?			
5.	What might happen if the population of pandas grew quickly?			

Summarize and Paraphrase

Paraphrasing means restating something you read in your own words. Paraphrasing can help you understand and remember what you read. Read each of the following passages from "Plenty About Pandas" and rewrite them in your own words.

1. From the article:	2. From the article:
Pandas, which can weigh up to 275 pounds, live mostly on bamboo. They each eat up to 33 pounds of bamboo every day!	Long ago, people thought pandas had magical powers. They were even kept as pets by kings. However, their stately history hasn't kept them safe. Giant pandas are in danger.
1. Your paraphrase:	**2. Your paraphrase:**

Comprehension Practice

Circle the letter of the best answer.

1. What belief did people long ago have about pandas?
   A. They lived underground.
   B. They had magical powers.
   C. They made bamboo grow.
   D. They were dangerous meat-eaters.

2. What is different about a panda's paws?
   A. It has only two toes.
   B. It cannot be used for walking.
   C. It has a special bone that works like a thumb.
   D. The skin on them is very thick.

3. What problem do pandas have in zoos?
   A. The population is growing too fast.
   B. They have trouble sleeping.
   C. There is not enough food.
   D. They have difficulty breeding.

4. What makes up most of a panda's diet?
   A. honey
   B. tree bark
   C. bamboo
   D. fish

5. What is one way in which people are trying to save pandas?
   A. protecting the forests where they live
   B. moving them all into zoos
   C. keeping them as pets
   D. collecting extra bamboo for them

La Torre di Pisa

Leaning Tower of Pisa

You don't speak Italian? La Torre di Pisa means "the Tower of Pisa." It has long been known as the Leaning Tower, for the obvious reason that it leans to one side.

Pisa is a town in central Italy. Work began on this bell tower in 1173. By the time the third floor was done, the tower had begun to sink on one side. Work was stopped for 99 years. In 1272, four more floors were added. They were built at an angle. People hoped this would make up for the tilt. But work was stopped again in 1301. It wasn't until 1372 that the last floor was added and the bell put in the top.

For centuries, people studied how to fix the tilt. In 1934, Italian ruler Benito Mussolini ordered that the tower be straightened. Tons of cement were poured into the base of the tower. The results were bad. The tower sank further into the soft soil.

In 1964, Italy asked for help. It was clear that the old tower was never going to be straight. But the greater danger was that it would eventually fall over. Experts from around the world met to talk about ways to keep the tower standing.

In 1989, the tower was closed to the public. For 11 years, work was done to make the tower sturdy. In 2001, the tower was reopened. With the help of thick cables, the tower is now stable. People from all over the world still visit the famous Leaning Tower of Pisa.

Before Reading

- Where is Pisa?
- Where have you seen the Leaning Tower?

During Reading

- What was the tower's purpose?
- How long did it take to build the tower?

After Reading

- What are some reasons the old tower still stands?
- Why do you think people have long been interested in fixing and protecting the Leaning Tower?

Vocabulary

angle: the difference in direction of two surfaces

experts: people who know a lot about a particular subject

Identify Cause and Effect

Fill in the missing cause and effect in the chart. Then write two other cause-effect relationships in the space provided.

Cause	Effect
The tower began to sink after the third floor was completed.	
	Tons of cement were poured into the base of the tower, and it sank further.

#10120 Reading Comprehension—Level F   *Teacher Created Materials, Inc.*

Identify Sequence

Write the following events below in the order in which they occurred.

Benito Mussolini ordered "repairs" that caused the tower to sink more.
The last floor was built, and the bell was put in place.
The tower was closed, and thick cables were added to support it.
The tower was reopened to the public.
The Italian government asked experts from around the world to help.
Work begins on the tower.
Four floors are added, built at an angle.
The tower begins to sink to one side as the third floor is completed.

1.

2.

3.

4.

5.

6.

7.

8.

Comprehension Practice

Circle the letter of the best answer.

1. When did work begin on the tower for the first time?
   A. 1301
   B. 1173
   C. 1272
   D. 1934

2. What was the original purpose for the Tower of Pisa?
   A. It was a watchtower to protect the city.
   B. It was a tourist attraction.
   C. It was a bell tower.
   D. It was a church.

3. Who ordered that the tower be straightened in 1934?
   A. building experts from around the world
   B. Benito Mussolini
   C. Italian scientists
   D. the artist who designed the tower

4. Why did the Italian government seek help from other experts?
   A. They wanted to add additional floors to the tower.
   B. Tourists were no longer interested in seeing the tower.
   C. They wanted to tear down the tower and build a new one.
   D. The tower was in danger of falling over.

5. What holds the tower steady today?
   A. columns that prop it up on one side
   B. magnets
   C. thick steel cables
   D. extra cement in the base

Where the Big Cats Roam

Before Reading

- What are some big cats?
- Where have you seen wild cats?

During Reading

- Where do wild cats live?
- What cats live in which climates?

After Reading

- What kind of wild cat would you like to be?
- How do you think wild cats are like domestic cats?

w Leopard

There are 37 types of wild cats in the world. They can be found in snowy mountains, deserts, grasslands, and rain forests. Cats of all shapes and sizes roam the earth.

Rain Forests: Most wild cats are found in the tropics, where the weather is warm all year. Rain forests provide a home for jaguars, leopards, pumas, and tigers. Pumas and jaguars are found in the Americas. Tigers and leopards are found in forests from Siberia to Africa and Southeast Asia.

Grasslands: The rich grasslands of Africa are home to several big cats. During the wet season, the land is green and partly flooded. It is very dry in summer. Lions and cheetahs live in these grasslands. Most lions are found in Africa and a small part of India. Cheetahs are also mostly in Africa, but some live in other places, too.

Mountains: Few cats live in harsh mountain areas. Only the snow leopard lives high up in the frozen Asian mountains. Its thick fur coat keeps it warm in freezing weather.

Deserts: Some smaller wild cats live in rocky, desert places. The bobcat, jaguar, and lynx are the most common wild cats in these arid places.

Tiger

Lynx

Vocabulary

arid: dry

roam: to go from place to place; wander

tropics: a warm, wet region immediately north and south of the equator

Compare and Contrast

Use the diagram below to compare the types of cats that live in Asia and Africa. In the circle on the left, write cats that live only in Africa. In the circle on the right, list cats that live only in Asia. In the area where the two circles overlap, write cats that live in both Asia and Africa.

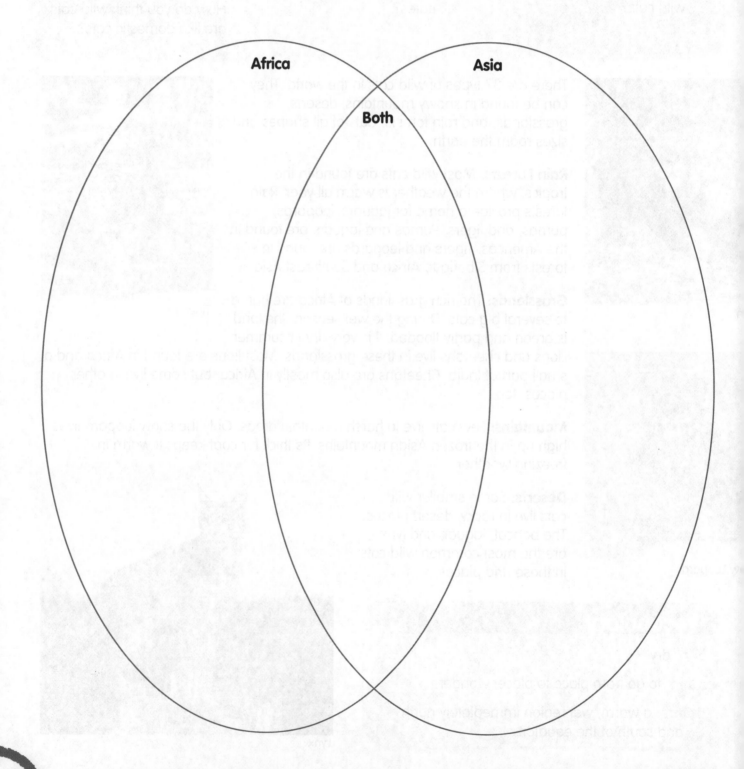

Africa   **Both**   **Asia**

Use Text Organizers

The chart shows the headings in the article. Each heading identifies an area where certain cats live. Use the article to place the cats named into the appropriate habitat.

Rain Forests	Grasslands	Mountains	Deserts

Comprehension Practice

Circle the letter of the best answer.

1. How many types of wild cats are there?
   A. 70
   B. 57
   C. 37
   D. 17

2. Most wild cats are found in what type of area?
   A. arctic
   B. tropical
   C. wetland
   D. desert

3. Which of the following are you unlikely to find in a desert?
   A. lion
   B. bobcat
   C. lynx
   D. jaguar

4. What type of cat is best adapted to life on an icy mountain?
   A. white lion
   B. puma
   C. lynx
   D. snow leopard

5. Where do most lions live?
   A. Asia
   B. South America
   C. Africa
   D. Australia

Not So Different

Before Reading

- What do best friends do?
- Are family members usually more alike or different?

During Reading

- How are the two girls alike?
- How are the girls different?

After Reading

- How are your cousins different from you?
- How can it be good to be close to cousins and other family members?

Vocabulary

conversation: a discussion or chat among a few people

hazel: light or greenish brown

oboe: a type of wind instrument

petite: small or short

Fran and Karen are cousins and best friends. They both have black eyes, but otherwise they look completely different. Fran is blonde and tall, while Karen is petite and has brown hair.

Fran always says Karen is lucky because she can walk to school. Fran has to take the bus. On rainy days, Karen carries her umbrella, while Fran just wears a raincoat. Neither of the girls likes rain, but they both love snowy winters.

In the mornings, the girls meet in the lunchroom to chat. They talk about what their families did the night before. Karen's family usually watches a movie after dinner. Fran's family prefers TV, but sometimes her mom or dad reads aloud to the family. Karen has two brothers and Fran has three. Karen's parents are both teachers, while Fran's parents own a pet store.

During their conversation, Fran and Karen also talk a lot about things they do at school. Karen likes reading and writing, while Fran looks forward to art class. They love using their imaginations, but they do it in different ways.

Both girls love music. Karen plays the flute and Fran plays the oboe. Sometimes they make up songs of their own or play along together to songs on the radio.

The two girls also talk about what they'd like to be and where they'd like to go. Karen wants to be in business and travel to Europe. Fran wants to be a scientist and study whales. But until then, Karen and Fran want to enjoy school and keep having their morning chats.

Compare and Contrast

Use the diagram below to compare the two girls in "Not So Different." In the circle on the left, write details about Fran. In the circle on the right, write details about Karen. In the area where the two circles overlap, write details that the two girls have in common.

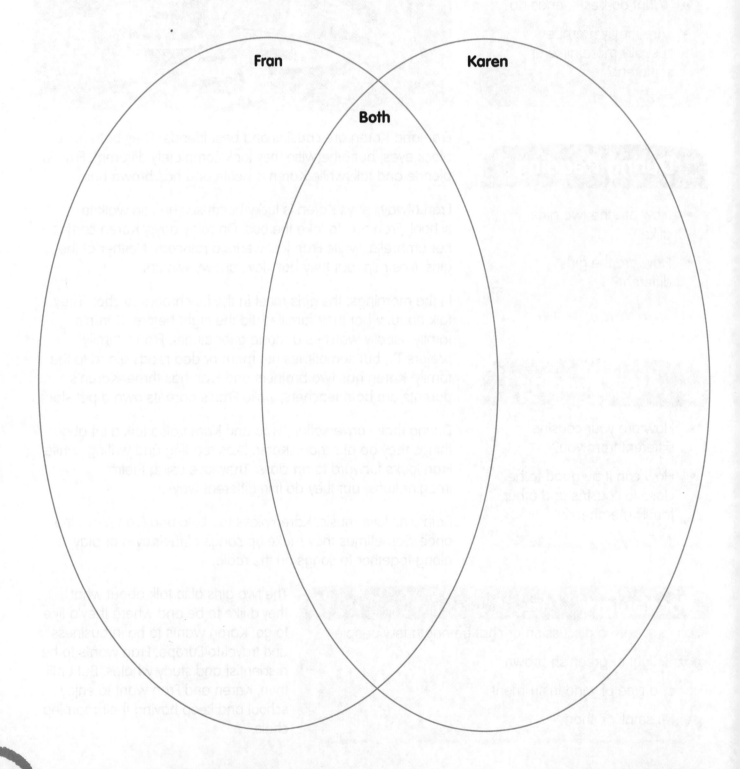

Fran

Karen

Both

Summarize and Paraphrase

Paraphrasing means restating something you read in your own words. Paraphrasing can help you understand and remember what you read. Read each of the following passages from "Not So Different" and rewrite them in your own words.

---

1. From the story:

Fran always says Karen is lucky because she can walk to school. Fran has to take the bus. On rainy days, Karen carries her umbrella, while Fran just wears a raincoat.

2. From the story:

Karen's family usually watches a movie after dinner. Fran's family prefers TV, but sometimes her mom or dad reads aloud to the family.

1. Your paraphrase:

2. Your paraphrase:

Comprehension Practice

Circle the letter of the best answer.

1. Why does Fran think Karen is lucky?
   A. Karen has a nice raincoat.
   B. Karen gets to walk to school.
   C. Karen has blonde hair.
   D. Karen plays the oboe really well.

2. What do both girls dislike?
   A. snow
   B. riding the bus
   C. rain
   D. math class

3. What do Fran's parents do for a living?
   A. watch movies
   B. teach at school
   C. study whales
   D. own a pet shop

4. What subjects does Karen like best?
   A. math and geography
   B. reading and writing
   C. science and math
   D. art and gym

5. What is an activity the girls do together?
   A. play music
   B. study whales
   C. watch TV
   D. ride the school bus

The Litterbusters

Before Reading

- What is litter?
- How do you feel about people who litter?

During Reading

- Where does the story take place?
- What happens after Carla and Brian write their letter?

After Reading

- Why do you think people in the neighborhood signed the letter?
- Do you think it's important to keep your town clean? Why or why not?

Carla was riding the public bus with her older brother, Brian. It was pretty hot outside, so they decided to get off the bus and buy some cold drinks. They got their refreshments and took a walk down the street.

As they waited at the crosswalk, they saw a fancy new car pull up. As they admired the car, the passenger door opened a bit and out rolled an empty juice bottle. Then the light turned green and the car sped off.

Carla and Brian could hardly believe it. Who would deliberately put trash in the middle of the street? Brian noticed all the other garbage in gutters and on sidewalks. He explained to Carla how much he hated litter and how lazy it was to be a "litter bug." They decided that they had to get their neighborhood cleaned up.

When they got home, Carla and Brian wrote a letter.

They suggested that the city put public trashcans on every corner. They described how they felt about people littering in their town. They wrote that they wanted to see the streets and sidewalks cleaned up. They even had everyone in the neighborhood sign the letter. Then Brian mailed it to the mayor.

A few weeks later, Brian told Carla he wanted to show her something. He took his sister for a walk up the street. What do you think they saw? There were new trashcans on every corner and hardly any litter on the sidewalks!

The mayor had listened to them. Carla and Brian were happy and proud. They decided they would always help keep their town clean.

Vocabulary

admire: to have respect for a person or object

deliberately: on purpose, not accidentally

neighborhood: the specific area in which someone lives

Identify Author's Purpose and Viewpoint

Picture each scene in your mind. Write details about what you see.

1. What reasons might the author have had for writing "The Litterbusters"?

_____

_____

_____

_____

_____

_____

_____

_____

_____

2. Why do you think the author wrote this selection? Cite specific parts of the story.

_____

_____

_____

_____

_____

_____

_____

_____

_____

Analyze Plot Structure

Fill in the chart. Identify the elements of the plot.

Conflict/Problem
Action Leading to Solving the Problem
Resolution/Outcome

Comprehension Practice

Circle the letter of the best answer.

1. What are Carla and Brian doing at the beginning of the story?
   A. drinking juice
   B. riding their bikes
   C. writing a letter
   D. riding the bus

2. What did the people in the fancy new car put in the street?
   A. a new trashcan
   B. a letter for the mayor
   C. a juice bottle
   D. a paper bag

3. What does Brian call people who put trash on the ground?
   A. litter bugs
   B. garbage bugs
   C. trash bugs
   D. litter lovers

4. Who signed the letter?
   A. the people in the car
   B. the school principal
   C. the mayor
   D. the people in the neighborhood

5. How do Brian and Carla feel at the end?
   A. angry
   B. proud
   C. concerned
   D. sorry

Elephant and Woolly Mammoth: Are They the Same?

Woolly Mammoth

African Elephant

Asian Elephant

Before Reading

- What is a woolly mammoth?
- What do you know about elephants?

During Reading

- How are elephants like or unlike mammoths?
- How are the two elephant types different?

After Reading

- Why do you think mammoths became extinct?
- Do you think elephants could become extinct? Why or why not?

The woolly mammoth roamed Earth from about 2 million years ago until 9,000 years ago. Elephants are related to mammoths. They are similar to mammoths in many ways.

The biggest difference between the elephant and mammoth is hair. Mammoths lived during the last ice age. They had thick fur to help keep them warm. The African elephant lives in hot, dry places. The Asian elephant lives in warm, moist areas. Because they don't have to worry about keeping warm, they don't need the same furry coat.

Mammoths had long trunks. They were not quite as long as the African elephant's trunk. They were more like the size of the Asian elephant's trunk, perhaps just a bit longer. Like elephants, mammoths were herbivores. That means they didn't eat meat. Just as you may have seen elephants do, mammoths used their trunks to drink and to grab food. They could eat up to 600 pounds (272 kilograms) of food every day!

Both male and female mammoths had huge, curved tusks. Male and female African elephants also have long tusks. Female Asian elephants don't have any tusks at all.

Mammoths had large ears, but they were not as big as those of elephants now. The African elephant has huge ears. They help get rid of body heat, keeping the elephant cooler. As you can see, elephants and mammoths are a lot alike, but not the same!

Vocabulary

herbivore: a plant-eating animal

ice age: a period of time when temperatures are much colder than average

Use Prior Knowledge and Make Connections

Answer these questions about the selection.

1. What is the topic of the selection?

   _____

2. What do you think of when you read the title? What does the title remind you of?

   _____

   _____

   _____

3. What do you think of when you look at the pictures? What do the pictures remind you of? How are they related?

   _____

   _____

   _____

4. What are some things you already know about mammoths? How did you learn these things?

   _____

   _____

   _____

5. What are some things you already know about elephants? How did you learn these things?

   _____

   _____

   _____

Compare and Contrast

Fill in the chart below to see how mammoths, African elephants, and Asian elephants are alike and how they are different.

	Woolly Mammoth	African Elephant	Asian Elephant
The weather where they live			
Hair			
Trunk			
Tusks			
Ears			
Food			

Comprehension Practice

Circle the letter of the best answer.

1. What modern animals are most similar to woolly mammoths?
   A. hippos
   B. saber-tooth tigers
   C. elephants
   D. giraffes

2. Which animal has the longest trunk?
   A. mammoth
   B. African elephant
   C. Asian elephant
   D. They're all alike.

3. Which animals do not have tusks?
   A. female mammoths
   B. female African elephants
   C. all Asian elephants
   D. female Asian elephants

4. Which animal has the smallest ears?
   A. female Asian elephant
   B. mammoth
   C. African elephant
   D. male Asian elephant

5. How much food could a mammoth eat per day?
   A. 100 pounds
   B. 60 pounds
   C. 600 pounds
   D. 1,000 pounds

Comprehension Review: Vocabulary—Word Meaning

Read each sentence. Use the information in the sentence to choose the meaning for the underlined word. Mark the answer.

1. The <u>flightless</u> penguins are birds that can only walk or swim.
   A. cold
   B. unlikely to use their wings
   C. unable to fly
   D. waddling

2. The <u>irate</u> customer turned and stamped out of the store in a huff.
   A. unhappy
   B. angry
   C. careless
   D. discourteous

3. Ben felt <u>drowsy</u> and decided to retire for the night.
   A. alert
   B. sleepy
   C. ill
   D. smart

4. Jason had to <u>adjust</u> to the darkness when the lights went out.
   A. adapt
   B. blink
   C. eliminate
   D. see

5. Her <u>contribution</u> to the charity auction was some antique jewelry.
   A. bid
   B. purchase
   C. reference
   D. donation

Comprehension Review: Vocabulary—Opposites

Read each sentence. Choose the word that means the opposite of the underlined word. Mark the answer.

1. The museum <u>received</u> the painting as a gift.
   - **A.** wrapped
   - **B.** sold
   - **C.** accepted
   - **D.** donated

2. The <u>saturated</u> soil could not hold another drop of water.
   - **A.** arid
   - **B.** wet
   - **C.** dripping
   - **D.** sandy

3. All other minerals can scratch talc, the <u>softest</u> mineral.
   - **A.** most difficult
   - **B.** flakiest
   - **C.** hardest
   - **D.** purest

4. Sitting quietly listening to music <u>soothed</u> the Mukluk.
   - **A.** calmed
   - **B.** agitated
   - **C.** focused
   - **D.** awoke

5. The couch looked oversized, even <u>gigantic</u>, in the small room.
   - **A.** large
   - **B.** diminutive
   - **C.** gross
   - **D.** spectacular

Comprehension Review: Vocabulary—Content Clues

Read each sentence. Use the information in the sentence to choose the best word to complete the sentence. Mark the answer.

1. Many species of birds ____ to warmer climates as winter approaches.
   A. leave
   B. migrate
   C. swim
   D. commute

2. Few plants grow in that ____, dry desert.
   A. barren
   B. fertile
   C. oasis
   D. green

3. Chameleons ____ themselves by changing their color to blend in with their surroundings.
   A. apply
   B. differentiate
   C. camouflage
   D. imitate

4. The clues made Tony ____ that someone was planning a surprise for him.
   A. identify
   B. positive
   C. answer
   D. suspect

5. Bookshelves lined the narrow ____ in the library.
   A. books
   B. roadway
   C. aisles
   D. video room

Comprehension Review: Sentence Completion

One word does not fit in the sentence. Use the sentence clues to choose that word. Mark the word that does NOT fit.

1. The wooly mammoth was a ____ prehistoric animal that looked like a hairy elephant.
   - A. huge
   - B. gigantic
   - C. petite
   - D. large

2. The streets were a mess with ____ strewn everywhere.
   - A. litter
   - B. gardens
   - C. garbage
   - D. trash

3. The twins were ____ in every way except one was taller than the other.
   - A. identical
   - B. alike
   - C. similar
   - D. distinctive

4. The candidate ____ to all of the reporters' questions.
   - A. replied
   - B. delegated
   - C. responded
   - D. answered

5. The lack of affordable sites ____ my plans to open a second store.
   - A. assisted
   - B. thwarted
   - C. foiled
   - D. checked

Comprehension Review:
Main Idea

Read each story. Mark the sentence that tells the main idea.

1. The line for the movie was really long. It started at the front door of the movie theater. It snaked down the street and around the corner. My guess is that at least 300 people were waiting in line.

   A. The line for the movie was really long.
   B. It started at the front door of the movie theater.
   C. It snaked down the street and around the corner.
   D. My guess is that at least 300 people were waiting in line.

2. The words **bow** and **bow** are spelled alike but pronounced differently. **Bow** rhymes with **how**, but **bow** rhymes with **toe**. They have different meanings. The words **bow** and **bow** are homographs.

   A. The words **bow** and **bow** are spelled alike but pronounced differently.
   B. **Bow** rhymes with **how**, but **bow** rhymes with **toe**.
   C. They have different meanings.
   D. The words **bow** and **bow** are homographs.

3. Many different animals hibernate during the winter months. Some birds hibernate off and on throughout the cold months. Groundhogs and bats are mammals that hibernate. Frogs are examples of amphibians that hibernate.

   A. Some birds hibernate off and on throughout the cold months.
   B. Many different animals hibernate during the winter months.
   C. Groundhogs and bats are mammals that hibernate.
   D. Frogs are examples of amphibians that hibernate.

Comprehension Review:
Stated Details

Read the paragraph. Use the information in the paragraph to complete the sentences. Mark the answer.

The number and variety of insects are amazing. Scientists have identified about 1 million different kinds of insects. Some of these are pests or even enemies. The boll weevils destroy large amounts of cotton each year. The Hessian flies can damage wheat crops, and the corn earworms destroy ears of corn. Some clothes moths and carpet beetles will chew through clothes and carpets, ruining them. Termites can destroy wood joists, furniture, and paper by dining on them. Some types of mosquitoes can transmit diseases such as malaria, yellow fever, West Nile virus, and encephalitis. Dysentery and cholera can be spread by houseflies. Not all insects are harmful. Many actually are helpful. All are a part of the living world.

1. Hessian flies can destroy _____.
   A. wheat crops   B. cotton   C. corn   D. wood

2. Scientists have identified about _____ kinds of insects.
   A. 10,000   B. 100,000   C. 1 million   D. 10 million

3. Carpets can be ruined by a type of _____.
   A. boll weevil   B. beetle   C. mosquito   D. fly

4. Houseflies may spread _____.
   A. encephalitis   B. yellow fever   C. malaria   D. dysentery

5. Termites can destroy furniture made from _____.
   A. wood   B. steel   C. glass   D. vinyl

Comprehension Review: Classify/Categorize

Read each group of words. Mark the word that does NOT fit in the same category as the other words.

1. **A.** onion
   B. apple
   C. carrot
   D. sweet potato

2. **A.** stream
   B. ocean
   C. river
   D. creek

3. **A.** ant
   B. bee
   C. wasp
   D. worm

4. **A.** folk tale
   B. biography
   C. novel
   D. short story

5. **A.** ship
   B. helicopter
   C. hot-air balloon
   D. airplane

6. **A.** daisy
   B. maple
   C. elm
   D. oak

7. **A.** almond
   B. pecan
   C. peach
   D. cashew

8. **A.** gram
   B. liter
   C. inch
   D. meter

9. **A.** smile
   B. applaud
   C. grimace
   D. frown

10. **A.** butte
    B. hill
    C. mountain
    D. plain

Comprehension Review: Sequence

Read the paragraph. Then answer the questions.

Bocce is a lawn-bowling game popularized in Italy. In the game, each of two teams get four balls. A team's goal is to get its balls as close to the target ball, or pallina, as possible. To decide which team will go first, a coin is tossed. The winner of the coin toss chooses which color of balls it will use. Play begins when a player from that team throws out the pallina. Then the same player rolls or tosses his or her bocce, trying to get as close to the pallina as possible. A player from the opposing team then takes a turn. The team whose ball is farther from the pallina takes the next turn. It continues until it runs out of balls or one of its balls rolls closer to the pallina than the other team's ball. Whenever a team gets closer, it is the next team's turn. When both teams have played all balls, players check to see which team has the ball closest to the pallina. The team with the closest ball scores one point for each of its balls that is closer than the nearest ball of the other team. A new round then begins. Usually a game is ended when a team scores 16 points.

1. What happens first in the game of bocce?
   A. One team rolls a ball.
   B. A player tosses the pallina.
   C. A point is scored.
   D. A coin is tossed to see which team goes first.

2. What happens immediately after both teams have played their four balls?
   A. The pallina is thrown out.
   B. The round ends.
   C. The teams check to see which team has the closest balls.
   D. The opposing team rolls its first ball.

3. What happens next after a team gets one of its balls closest to the pallina?
   A. The game is over.
   B. The other team takes a turn.
   C. The team continues its turn.
   D. The pallina is moved.

4. When is the first bocce ball thrown?
   A. before the coin toss
   B. before a team chooses the color of balls it will use
   C. after the pallina is thrown
   D. after 16 points are scored

Comprehension Review: Plot, Setting, Characters

Read the selection. Use the information to answer each question.

Mark the answers.

On Thursday after school, Shelby stepped out on the stage in the school's auditorium. She waited for the piano player to begin playing, and then she began to sing. Just seconds later, a voice from the darkened auditorium said, "Thank you very much; next please." Shelby was disappointed. She desperately wanted a leading role in the school production of "Sound of Music." But she was dismissed from the stage before she had a chance to truly show her singing ability. Shelby watched and listened as other students auditioned. Some were allowed to finish the entire song. Shelby feared that she would not get a part in the play. Then groups of students were called on stage to demonstrate dancing ability. Shelby thought her group did fine. Now the only thing left to do was to wait for the list of cast members to be posted on Tuesday. Finally Tuesday came, and Shelby checked the list. She hoped to at least get a part as a bit player, but her name wasn't on the chorus list. She hung her head and started to walk away. Then Cathy called out. "Shelby, you got the part of Liesl." Shelby couldn't believe it. She did get an important role.

1. Where does the story take place?

    A. school auditorium

    B. professional theater

    C. backstage

    D. classroom

2. When does the story take place?

    A. before class

    B. Saturday morning

    C. after school

    D. during study hour

3. Who is the main character?

    A. piano player

    B. Cathy

    C. Liesl

    D. Shelby

4. What does Shelby do at the beginning of the story?

    A. dances with a group

    B. waits for the cast list to be posted

    C. sings on stage

    D. watches others audition

5. How does the story end?

    A. Shelby doesn't get a part in the play.

    B. Shelby gets an important part in the play.

    C. Shelby is appointed a stagehand.

    D. Shelby quits the play.

Comprehension Review:
Predict

Read each paragraph. Use the information to predict what will happen. Mark the answer.

1. Sharon had been saving her babysitting money to buy a new bike. She counted her cash. She still needed $15.00. She had no jobs scheduled for today. Then Mrs. Moreno called to ask her to baby-sit. What will Sharon do?

   A. go to the library

   B. baby-sit

   C. meet friends at a store

   D. stay home

2. Oren read the directions and took the meal out of its box. He poked a hole in the plastic wrap, put the meal in the microwave, and punched in the numbers for the time. What will Oren do next?

   A. open another meal

   B. feed his fish

   C. start the microwave

   D. clear dishes off the table

3. Michael saw flashes of lightning. Then he heard the rumble of thunder in the distance. Soon the sky darkened and the wind picked up. A drizzle began to fall. What happened next?

   A. The sun came out.

   B. Michael went to bed for the night.

   C. A rainbow appeared.

   D. It began to rain very hard.

4. Chari bought her younger brother the neatest toy for a birthday surprise. She wrapped the gift and tied a bow around it. She didn't want her brother to see the gift before his party. What happens next?

   A. Chari gives the gift to her brother.

   B. Chari hides the gift.

   C. Chari shows the gift to her dad.

   D. Chari opens the gift.

Comprehension Review:
Make Inferences

Read the sentences. Use the information to make inferences. Mark your answer.

1. Dad served Jake some lasagna and salad. Then they talked about what their day had been like. Jake told Dad that after school he and Ben played basketball at the recreation center. What meal were Jake and Dad enjoying together?

   A. breakfast

   B. midmorning snack

   C. lunch

   D. dinner

2. Kristen couldn't wait to kick off her shoes and flop on her bed. It had been a long day. She walked into the lobby of her building and climbed three flights of stairs. Finally she was on her floor. She unlocked her door and threw the keys on a table near the entryway. She was home at last. Where does Kristen live?

   A. in a house

   B. in an apartment

   C. in a hotel

   D. in a basement

3. The third-grade teacher had the students number their papers from 1 to 20. Then she said a word, used it in a sentence, and said the word again. The students then wrote the word. They wrote 20 words and then the test was over. What kind of test did the students take?

   A. a math test

   B. a reading test

   C. a spelling test

   D. a music test

4. My dad worked part-time when he was in college. Every morning, he would give customers menus and take their orders. Dad said he often made $30.00 in tips. Where did Dad work?

   A. an office

   B. in a clothing store

   C. in a restaurant

   D. on a bus

Comprehension Review:
Cause and Effect

Read each sentence. Mark the cause or effect for the sentence.

1. Jeff put an ice cube in his soup. What is the effect?
   A. The soup boiled.
   B. The soup spilled.
   C. The soup was put back in the pot.
   D. The soup got cooler.

2. The doctor puts a cast on Sam's arm. What is the cause?
   A. Sam's arm has healed.
   B. Sam cut his arm.
   C. Sam liked the way casts look.
   D. Sam has a broken arm.

3. Terry's bike has a flat tire. What is the effect?
   A. Terry gets a new bike.
   B. Terry fixes the tire.
   C. Terry has the brakes on her bike adjusted.
   D. Terry rides her bike.

4. The bean plant was not given water. What was the effect?
   A. The plant grew quickly.
   B. The plant died.
   C. The plant blossomed.
   D. The plant needed less sunshine.

5. Tricia was elected president of the sixth grade. What was the cause?
   A. Tricia got more votes than other candidates.
   B. Tricia received fewer votes than anyone else.
   C. Tricia ran for class treasurer.
   D. Tricia was promoted to seventh grade.